IN THE CO

Ronald Walsh R.N.

IN THE COMPANY OF HEROES

Matador
9 De Montfort Mews
Leicester LE1 7FW, UK
Tel: (+44) 116 255 9312 / 9311
Fax: (+44) 116 255 9323
Email: books@troubador.co.uk
Web: www.troubador.co.uk/matador

ISBN 1 904744 47 8

Typeset in 11pt Plantin by Troubador Publishing Ltd, Leicester, UK
Printed by Cromwell Press Ltd, Trowbridge, Wilts

Matador is an imprint of Troubador Publishing Ltd

Dedicated to my brother John Walsh

CONTENTS

INTRODUCTION

This book has been written by and is about sailors, and it has been written by one who could be said to epitomise all the matelots who joined the Royal Navy prior to World War II. All those who served their country during that traumatic time, and after it was all over.

Our country and the world will not see their like again, for it is no longer a navy of hammocks and heavy guns, battleships and rigid discipline – but one of computers, simulators, satellites and missiles... and mixed blessings.

Boys' training has also disappeared from among the Royal Navy's priorities, be that a good or a bad thing. There was much that was bad with the "good old Navy", and most has long gone. However, the men the navy made were of the right calibre to fight the bloody, slogging battles on oceans all over the world against a ruthless enemy of the type the British Nation has long fought and defeated over hundreds of years.

This story is by a man who Drake would have known, Nelson too. Today he is a veteran enjoying his leisure. Yesterday he was a young man fighting for King and Country, for the freedom we enjoy today, a freedom not quite understood; what it means and exactly how hard it was to retain, and how easy it is to lose. Ron Walsh is one among many thousands of seamen who were a small part of a very large fight. His experiences during the war, and following it during the uneasy peace, are typical of thousands of others' experiences. Yet memories fade quickly, so it is vitally important that the experiences of the 'ordinary' man who served on the front line are preserved for posterity. History is not just about those who are in important positions of authority and power – it is about the men and women who toil relentlessly, doing their duty without question.

Ron Walsh and his comrades fought, and alongside them many died. A different era, certainly, but we ignore the past at our peril, and ignore the lessons these men taught us to our everlasting shame. Each of them was a hero among heroes.

Chapter 1

BOY'S SERVICE

On 28th April 1969 I was discharged from the Royal Navy, time served. A lot of years had passed since I had entered as a Boy 2nd Class having travelled from my home at Lymington in the heart of the New Forest, and arrived at the main gate of H.MS.Pembroke, the Royal Navy's Barracks at Chatham on a cold winters day in 1936. That was the 20th November. On 14th February 1937 I left Chatham as a Boy 1st Class to join H.M.S. Wildfire and begin training in the Men's Service. Wildfire was a training 'ship' in Sheerness Dockyard where I learnt more about my chosen service until that too came to an end, and I found myself joining my first sea-going ship on 15th June 1937. She was the First World War battleship H.M.S. Iron Duke, tied up at South Railway Jetty in Portsmouth Harbour, and I was one of 20 boys in the Boys Mess-deck which was run with iron discipline by two Petty Officer Instructors, both of whom were always around and always shouting orders, urging us to "Move" or "Double Up", reinforced with ropes end stonikys. These were 18 inch long ropes with a 'Turks Head' knot on the business end. Used craftily, they could induce one to move much faster than one normally intended. We certainly knew all about it then!

We boys had a full and energetic daily routine which began at 6.30am when the lights would be switched on and we heard "Out you get, fall in on the jetty with your hammocks correctly lashed (7 turns) in ten minutes. "This routine was always the same, summer or winter, rain or shine. After inspection the duty Physical Training Instructor (PTI) would lead us on a jog around the dockyard. Dark or light it made no difference to him "to wake you up and make you

1

H.M.S. Iron Duke

more interested in the day ahead!" Upon our return to the ship it was up the gangway and down to the Mess for 'kye' ('Pussers' cocoa – a really thick stand-your-spoon-up-in-it drink), off with shoes and socks, roll up your trousers legs to the knees. Hoses were readied then for the ships crew to come up from breakfast to wash down, the beginning of their daily routine. We lads then went down for our breakfast which began our day of instructional classes.

During our time on board *Iron Duke* we were not allowed shore leave but six of us were sent to *H.M.S. Excellent* on nearby Whale Island to receive instruction on the 'Dumerrique', a device used in gunnery range finding. We had a great time living on the Island for a week, although at first the G. I.'s (Gunnery Instructors) insistence on everyone doubling everywhere during working hours was a little bit wearing and took some getting used to.

This was prior to World War Two when the Island boasted it's own zoo. There were exotic birds, lions, a couple of bears, penguins on their own pond near the parade ground. In those days RN ships would do commissions of 18 months or 2 years and 6 months abroad, during which time they would collect various creatures with a view to presenting them to Whale Island Zoo when they returned home. Of course, when war became imminent the zoo was shut down and the animals dispersed. Even so, there were occasional gifts, one of a baby reindeer, to various ships by foreign personnel during the war.

From Whale Island we had a further week away from the old *Iron Duke* during a stay in Gosport, at *Fort Gomer,* near Stokes Bay. It was run by members of the Royal Garrison Artillery, although why we were put there for five days I can't recall. I do remember that some of the rooms, piled high on top with concrete and earth, were running with damp and they were cold and dark, and to cap it all we were used to hammocks, and instead we had Army-style straw-filled 'bedding biscuits' to sleep on.

Back on board the *Iron Duke* we watched coaling take place, and what an experience that was. Coaling ship was a dirty business, an unenviable task undertaken by the 'black gang', who were soon filthy, being covered in coal dust. With the advent of engines run on oil instead of steam, the practice was discontinued, except for a few old merchant navy ships during hostilities. We did our first sea time on that battleship. She used to slip from the South Railway Jetty (where Queen Victoria's train used to arrive, and a boat would take her to Gosport's Royal Clarence Yard on her journey to the Isle of Wight) in the morning, and steam out of harbour to Spithead, off the Nab Tower, and either carry out seamanship exercises, or shoot from her 13.5-inch heavy guns.

I recall that first time when I and my companions went to sea to experience such a shoot. The big guns were trained out to sea towards the target, and our class instructor grouped us on the upper deck close behind the gun muzzles. When they fired the first salvo we would be able to watch the projectiles in flight, he said. Suddenly

3

the guns opened fire, and believe it or not, we had no desire to hang about after that – to see a stupid shell flying through the air.

After four months of quite intensive training on *H.MS.Iron Duke,* six of us received a draft to a brand new 'City Class ' cruiser to be named *H.MS. Glasgow* on 14th September 1937. She completed building and we had commissioned her in time for us to spend two weeks as 'Open Ship' at the Glasgow Empire Exhibition, after which we began our 'running in' and 'acceptance trials' at Portland and Weymouth, based at Portsmouth. I completed my initial training and was now rated Ordinary Seaman. I was very pleased because it meant I was now able to take normal shore leave, and 'Pompey' being only about 50 miles from my home in Lymington, New Forest, it was an ideal arrangement.

We sailed off to Portland and Weymouth for further trials. It was during our time in Weymouth Bay that there was a strange occurrence. It was a beautiful sunny morning and the ship was steaming in large circles within the bay, whilst the normal activity took place on the bridge. The usual people were there, such as the Chief Yeoman of Signals, Officer of the Watch, etc., plus the Captain. I was the Captain's runner, so I was also there close on his heels. The atmosphere on the bridge then began to change rapidly as the Captain and Navigating Officer began to exchange remarks – then the Captain gave an order to the Officer of the Watch (OOW), who passed the instruction down a voice pipe. It was now 11am, and we were about half a mile from crowded Weymouth beach, heading straight for it. We began to put on speed, our bows cleaving the water and bow wave rising higher and higher until we sped between two wooden piers and straight up the beach, burying our bows and midships into the sand, our stern jutting out into the sea. What a predicament for a brand new cruiser to be in, and well and truly stuck!

H.M.S.Glasgow refused to budge when her engines were driven astern, and messages were sent to Portland for help. Meanwhile, the

H.M.S. Glasgow

crew were told to go to the stern and all at the same time jump up and down – what a display the holiday makers got for free. Aeroplanes were now buzzing overhead taking photos for newspapers. Two destroyers had been dispatched to us and also a couple of tugs which continued the effort to re-float us. This was not accomplished until later that afternoon, when the tide was at its highest. There was no apparent damage to the hull, and so we were able to continue our trials. The story and pictures were plastered over the national and local papers next day. I was not very impressed with that fiasco, which seemed somehow to typify my growing view that the pre-war Navy was not much more than a pastime for some of its Officers. Nevertheless, I was in, and I was determined to make the best of it!

H.M.S. Glasgow was a lovely ship, brand new, immaculate wooden decks. A most comfortable vessel in every way, and this became more apparent as we completed our workup and steamed many miles at home and abroad. During Spain's Civil War we were at

5

Gibraltar, making visits on several occasions. Later we paid a courtesy call at Stavanger in Norway, where British forces would be in action in the near future. The crew during that first commission was a really good lot, and all things considered we were a happy ship. I had a couple of good shore-going pals by the name of 'Olly' Shepherd and Bill 'Whacker' Toombs. Many years after *Glasgow*, I tried to contact them, but to no avail, and I have no idea if they survived the war or are still around.

It was around mid-1938 and I was on a weekend leave at home in Lymington when my Dad asked me to have a look around when I got back to Portsmouth and see if I could find a car. If there was one I liked, he would buy it for me and make getting from ship to home, and vice versa, that much easier. I didn't need any encouragement, so when I was back on board I scanned newspaper advertisements in the *Portsmouth Evening News*. I found one for a 1931 Austin 7 'Ruby' Saloon car in very nice condition. It was at North End and cost £7. That sounded good to me, so off I went, and finding the house was soon with the owner in his garage as he pulled off the covering sheet. The car looked immaculate. The middle aged owner asked if I would like a test run and I agreed. He asked where I lived, said "Jump in", and off we went. Our run via Southampton to the New Forest went without incident. Dad got my older brother to take the car out and confirm all was well, and the deal was made. The chap was paid his money plus his train fare back to Portsmouth and I had my own transport.

I put in a request to the Captain of *Glasgow* to enable me to keep the car in the Dockyard, and that's when my problems began, because in those days only Officers had cars. Even Chiefs and Petty Officers rode bicycles, so there were no ratings' car parks nearby. When I came in front of the Captain he went to town on me. "Who do you think you are having your own transport, isn't public transport good enough?" There was nothing laid down in regulations on which he could base a refusal, but he made it quite clear that if I ever defaulted in getting back to the ship from home due to my use of the car then he would deal with me "in no uncertain manner Walsh!" Eventually, of course, I did trip up. Returning early one Monday morning, with my two 'oppos' who used to accompany me at weekends, the car had a puncture. It took 10 minutes to change the wheel, and it was asking too much to make up the time and we were now adrift. A reception committee was waiting when we arrived on board. My 'oppos' were 'case dismissed', but I was placed on "Commander's Report", who passed me upwards to "Captain's Report", which was what this was all about! As good as his word, the Captain handed down 14 days No 9's, which meant that for two weeks I had my leave stopped and was given extra work to do. Men under punishment also mustered three times daily. The ship was due to sail in 10 days time, to Canada, where she would escort the King and Queen across the Atlantic at the start of their Canadian Tour. This meant we would be away for three months.

It was not possible for me to get my car home because I could not leave the ship, and it couldn't stay in the dockyard as there were no parking facilities. I had no alternative but to ask to see the Captain and ask for five hours leave on Saturday to drive home and get the train back. He refused outright. I talked it over with my two chums, and with their help devised a plan. I would desert from the Royal Navy. It was beginning to bore me stiff anyway, and there was so much pettiness. It took a lot of working out. We were berthed at the South Railway Jetty and the gangway was manned at all times by a Royal Marine sentry. I had to get the car into Queen Street. The last 'liberty boat' was at 9pm, and so was the last "man under punishment" muster. I would need to be at both of them! Our planning paid off, so at 9pm on 6th January 1939 I deserted *H.MS. Glasgow* and the Navy.

My new life began with approximately 10 hours start before the next muster was due at 7.30am the following morning, when I would be discovered to be 'absent'. They never did get me, and I never did change my name! I drove my car to Pennington, part of

Lymington, where my brother John had his cycle shop, and I exchanged my car for a cycle and rode it through the night to Wincanton in Somerset to my other brother, Fred's place of work, a farm, where I stayed a short time. Fred was normally employed as an engineer with the Westland Aircraft Company of Yeovil. A branch had moved to the north of England, and until such times as he could join them there, he had taken temporary work on the farm which was 14 miles outside town.

I explained the situation to Fred, and a couple of days later he took me to see his employer, who decided to take me on for a trial period. I didn't have high hopes of lasting very long because the boss wanted a milker and he knew I hadn't a clue. He asked Fred to teach me, and meanwhile he would set about getting proper work cards for me, which I didn't have for obvious reasons. I never did manage to master the art of milking cows, the bloody animals always worked against me, and invariably I ended up on my backside in the muck gully.

With Fred's backing I managed to hold out, scanning the papers all the while, seeking a position of my own. Eventually I came across a 'wanted' advert for the position of butcher/driver/salesman with Denning Brothers of Yeovil, and so I wrote to apply for it, had an interview and was taken on. Butchery was new to me, but the boss said I would soon pick it up with the help of his head slaughter-man and his helpers. I was already a qualified driver.

It was one winter morning at 7.30am when I started the job and I could work overtime until 7pm if I was required. As I was still living at Fred's place, that meant getting up at 6am to peddle the 14 miles into Yeovil to get there in time. This was a six day week, and I got home at 9pm each night. It was worth it though, because the pay was terrific. On a Monday forenoon five of us would accompany Mr. Denning who, besides being the shop owner, was also a gentleman farmer with a large farm outside Yeovil and, on top of that, while I worked for him he was also Mayor of Yeovil.

8

The cattle market was close to the butcher's shop with the slaughterhouse behind, and Mr Denning would buy perhaps five steers, 15 pigs, three calves, and 12 sheep at the market, and we would drive them to the slaughterhouse and pen them until the afternoon. By Tuesday afternoon they would all be hanging up in the large walk-in refrigerator at the rear of the shop. Another shop, in Market Street, served as our cooked meats preparation room, where sausages were made and large ovens were filled with cooking steak & kidney pies. We used five 'Morris 8' delivery vans to take our produce out to customers during the latter half of the week. By Sunday I certainly needed my day of rest, before it was back into it again on Monday. I managed the cycling back and forth to and from work for two weeks then was able to secure my own 'digs' in Yeovil itself, which made things a whole lot more pleasant.

As I settled down with Dennings over a 10 month period it came about that I heard of a job available at a large carpet sales shop just around the corner from Market Street. I got the position and it was a great improvement as far as I was concerned, with better hours and more time off. When I had gone AWOL from *H.M.S.Glasgow* on 6th January 1939 I had no idea that World War II was looming. Had I done so I would probably have steered a different course and not deserted. However, when war was declared in September 1939 I had to think carefully about what it was I should be doing. Certainly I did not wish to back away from a war, but it was rumoured that the whole thing would be over by Christmas and so I resolved to carry on as before but, if necessary, join the war effort if circumstances changed for the worse.

On 5th March 1940 I would be 20 years old, so I registered, as required, and then was informed that I should attend an Army interview in Taunton. There I was seen by a Captain, who asked what my civilian occupation was, and when I told him that I was a driver, adding that I also had a licence to drive several different kinds of vehicle from car to motorcycle, and would appreciate his putting me down for that type of work, he agreed to write on the form what

I was best suited for. Meanwhile, I should wait at home for notification to arrive by post very shortly. Came the 15th April and the all important buff O.H.M.S. envelope arrived containing a letter directing me to report forthwith to the Liverpool Depot of the Queens Light Infantry, and to help me get there was a postal order for 5 shillings (25p) and a railway ticket to that city.

I felt let down and angry that the Officer's recommendation had been ignored and my skills were not appreciated. No way was I going to footslog around the world when I had already volunteered to drive around it!

I had one week to think over this new development, but really there was no other recourse than to make my way to Portsmouth and give myself up to the Navy, throwing myself on their tender mercy, although I expected little of that. I was a deserter and I had to take whatever punishment they gave me, for I did not wish to spend the rest of my life looking over my shoulder. I was a trained seaman after all, and the Navy could use me at sea right away (or after punishment anyway), so on 4th April 1940, some 15 months after leaving the Service, I entrained for Portsmouth. On arrival I made my way to the main gate, where a large crowd of civilians was watching a Royal Marine band playing for the sailors marching up and down the parade ground.

With shoulders to the fore I barged my way through the crush to a side gate where, from the small duty office an RPO (Regulating Petty Officer/Navy Policeman) put up an arm to stop me going through. "You can't come in here, Sir," he said, "unless you've got a pass. Have you a pass?"

"Sorry RPO but I haven't" I replied, to which he retorted "Then I suggest that you go away, Sir". So I did! I proceeded along Queen Street, where I found a cafe and drank a cup of coffee to mull over what to do next. There was nothing for it but to return and try another tack, a headlong assault to crack this little nut. After all, here was I, a deserter trying to get back in, and they wouldn't let me! The crowd was still there as I confronted the RPO.

"I want to come in." That was to the point!
"Civilians aren't allowed in." So I let him have it.
"I am not a civilian but a matelot."
"Then where is your uniform?"
"I am afraid I ditched it when I went ashore from *H.M.S. Glasgow* and never came back, about 14 months ago."

He exclaimed, "Bloody hell, stay where you are." A similar gasp came from the crowd, who had heard it all. The RPO called out the guard to the main gate, and I was marched away between the two of them across to the M.A.A.'s Office and was put in a cell of sorts in the main block to the rear of the main gate, where I was told I would remain until all that I had said was confirmed.

During the following afternoon an officer visited me and said that it had been confirmed that I was a deserter and my service documents were being requested so that I could properly be dealt with by Commodore *H.M.S. Victory*, who was Commodore Walker, RN. For the following 10 days I was kept busy in my cell, as well as scrubbing and polishing the passageways, and also being questioned so that all the facts could be presented when I appeared before the Commodore. I was an object of speculation among the Regulating Branch members (or 'crushers' as they were known), as to what I might eventually get when I was 'weighed off'. Some thought I would get 90 days and dishonourable discharge. Others had the idea I might be shot at dawn. Very nice!

The day came when I was marched in at the double between two armed guards, across the parade ground to the Commodore's Office, and was soon standing before him. He delved into my explanation, asking many questions, probing my reasons for my "Offence of Deserting From His Majesty's Royal Navy!" I explained all that had taken place to lead to my desertion, the difficulties with the car, and my having no alternative but to deal with them myself. He asked about the significance of the Army papers and rail ticket on his desk, and I explained that I had managed to do well outside, about my wanting to do war service, and that the Army had let me down eventually, and how I would go back after the war and continue my job. "Why", he asked, "did you not just carry on as a civilian and ignore the Army and the Navy; how come you are now standing before me defending this most serious charge of desertion." I explained that rather than become a 'foot slogger' in the Infantry, I was a trained sailor and would be of greater use in war doing my own job, and would cope with all that might happen by giving myself up and taking my punishment so that I could go on in the Navy. Twice more I was marched in front of the Commodore as he delved into my explanations and reasons, and weighed the pro's and con's and established it all in his mind. Eventually, I was told that on my next and final appearance I would be dealt with, and my sentence pronounced. Wheeled in front of Commodore Walker I stood to attention and waited for the axe to fall.

"I have carefully considered all the evidence of this case and in some parts I can understand your reaction to the Naval discipline that you may have thought was wrong or harsh at times. However, you did sign a contract when you joined the Royal Navy in 1936. Since you left us when it was peace-time the stricter routines are likely to alter with the time of war we now find ourselves in. You are a trained seaman, Walsh, and I feel that you can offer a lot of good service in the future. Also, though you found life much more pleasant and rewarding financially while you were away, you have acted correctly and given yourself up. You did not seek to hide by changing your name, and that is to your credit. I have been advised that we no longer shoot deserters, Walsh, and I also have been advised that I can give you a 'Kings Free Pardon' – and that is what I am going to do here. You have deserted in peace-time and voluntarily given yourself up when war happened. A Free Pardon in your case means that you will continue where you left off. You will retain your service number that you had when you left us, and will report yourself to the drafting office – doubtless they will very soon fix you up with a suitable draft. I do not need to remind you that I trust in the future years you will give of your best. Case dismissed!"

At that, the M.A.A. (Master At Arms) dismissed the two armed guards and I walked out a free man. I made my way to the Drafting Office and, after that, to the canteen for a cup of char!

Chapter 2

IN THE BEGINNING

My father had served in the Royal Navy for 27 years, fighting in both the Boer War and Great War of 1914–1918. Afterwards he had joined *H.M. Coastguard* and was based at Brook, Isle of Wight until moving just across the Solent to Lymington with his wife, three sons, and two daughters. It was Christmas 1919. This lovely town on the South Coast, in the heart of the New Forest lies on the Lymington River and is now, as it was then, a fine yachting centre with first-class facilities which included the Royal Lymington Yacht Club. The City of Southampton and towns of Bournemouth and Beaulieu are within easy reach.

Having to quickly find accommodation my parents settled first into a small cottage in Bath Road, although it was hardly suitable for a large family with boisterous children. Apparently the cottage had a somewhat notorious history for it was said locally that it had been well used by smugglers in days gone by. The Lymington River ran close by and steps led down to under-house cellars, the hallmark of a smugglers roost. A plaque now fixed to its front wall now attests to this as I found when recently visiting old haunts. It was into this house that I was born on 5th March 1920, about two months after the move from Brook, and it was soon afterwards that my parents found the ideal family home when they purchased two cottages which had been knocked into one at nearby Waterford. This afforded the family a detached property with four bedrooms and a long side garden. It was called Brook Cottage and had, in earlier days, been Waterford Post Office.

My first recollections are from when I was four years old and Dad was working for an auctioneer at Hythe, near Beaulieu whilst mum took in washing for various local families. Dried and ironed, the baskets of freshly laundered clothes be returned to their owners by my brothers on their way to school. I was enrolled in the New Street Church of England school which was about a mile and a quarter from home. My little sister and I had to walk, or more often run, to school as invariably we were late and had to get to New Street before the school bell sounded for 9am.

Everyday life for we younger siblings was fairly normal for those times. I began school at age five, though, because I hated it intensely. I would seek any excuse not to be there. There was little in the way of entertainment in the 1920s so we would play around lamp posts until called for supper and bed. When I was seven years of age my 22 year old brother had a wooden shed built in the garden, from which he opened a motorcycle and bicycle repair shop. From then on I spent many hours helping him, and he taught me all about cars and motorbike engines. This continued for a year.

By now I was in the choir at nearby All Saints Church, so that Sundays were filled with Morning and Evening Services, and Sunday School in the afternoon at the small Chapel in Woodside. I mentioned entertainment, and recall that we did have a radio which was really more of a nuisance due to the heavy re-fillable batteries it ran on, which had to be constantly re-charged. They would often run out of power at critical moments. There was also a Saturday afternoon matinee at the local 'Lyric' cinema, which was a popular diversion for 4 pence.

At age seven I joined the local sea-cubs and later on the 9th Lymington Sea Scouts, which was formed by Mr Robert Hole and run by Mr Claridge, two men from whom we learnt a great deal, including rope splicing, knots, rowing and sailing in the ex-Royal Navy whaler we had moored at the river side. Obviously, proximity to the river meant that we spent many hours on it or in its vicinity. Some weekends we sailed across the Solent to Gurnard or Yarmouth on the Island. Two week summer camps were special to us. I recall one where we also spent two weeks on board a 'long-boat' or barge on the Kennet and Avon Canal. During one such 'camp', moving from Devizes, through Hungerford, Newbury and Reading, and returning the same way, our barge was drawn by a large horse led along a pathway by it's minder. A large rope led from the barge post to the horse's harness as he steadily plodded along taking the strain.

My brother John, who would also join the Navy, made me my own motorbike, an old BSA with round petrol tank and 'straight-up' gear stick. By the time I was 12 he had also taught me to drive a car as well!

I was about eight when there came a great change in our way of life. My parents inherited a large sum of money, the origin of which still remains a mystery to me. The first I knew that life would be different from now on was when a representative of a building firm called 'Osman & Tuton' began to call regularly at the cottage with plans, which were spread out on the kitchen table and studied by the adults. Satisfied with all the changes being asked for, the plans were finalised, and over the next weeks work began on the footings of the new house which would be built on a site with unobstructed views across to the Isle of Wight. We, by that I mean my younger sister and I, were told nothing, while our three elder brothers and remaining sister at home knew it all. Eventually, we pried the information from them that it would be a big house from which we could watch the big liners entering and leaving Southampton Water. It would be to our parent's design, and was to be situated in All Saints Road, around the corner. Tall trees in a nearby field stood like sentinels overlooking the new property, but eight had to be cut down to allow work to begin. It was an impressive sight as it grew into a double-fronted detached house, perched up on high ground which was covered by grass and flanked by trees. Over 70 years later it stands proudly among its neighbours. The pathways were mainly laid by my brothers and they also constructed the wooden sheds.

17

School was still not my favourite pastime, and my father was pushing me to go to Greenwich School in London where my elder brother Bob had been educated, and from which he joined the Navy. It was a boarding school run by the Navy for the sons of, or relatives of, former sailors. Bob had told me about his time there, and it all sounded more strict than I would like to commit myself to at the age of thirteen.

When my 13th birthday arrived it was 1933 and dad took me to 'Figures' Bicycle Shop in Lymington High Street to buy me a new Raleigh 3-speed bike, complete with saddle-bag. A couple of months later, I decided that I would leave home and see something of the big wide world. I bought myself a tent and other items I would need on the road, strapped everything to the bike and, at around midnight one night, off I went pedalling into the night having no idea where I was going. By dawn I was approaching Devizes, in Wiltshire. A place to stop and eat breakfast was soon found, and as I sat I began to make some plans for the day ahead. Nothing came to mind, so I just set off again.

Before long, I came upon a travelling fair being erected near the town centre on a huge bit of land, which has its own wall and large side gate. From a well, some fairground folk were hand-winding a bucket of water. At my vantage point opposite the fair entrance, I sat on the bike which was propped against the wall and watched the various swings and stalls being erected. I stayed there until noon. Among the various people coming out to the well, I noticed one woman, middle-aged and gypsy-looking, accompanied by a young girl who appeared about my own age, so I went over and joined them, and helped get their water up and carry it back to their caravan. They operated a sweet stall with nick-nacks and snacks, which they had set up just inside the gate. The mother, Mary, told me that they didn't belong to the fair but, like most stall-holders, they travelled with it and paid the fair boss, Mr Jack Jennings, rent for the privilege of trading when the fair was in full swing. It was past noon and I told Mary and her daughter Rosita that I was going to a cafe for a meal. Back at the fair things were getting a lot busier, and people were shouting orders as they erected familiar rides while a fairground-organ played popular songs of the day. The show people were adept at getting set up ready for opening times, and it was fascinating watching it being done. It was open at 6pm and shut at midnight!

At about 2pm that afternoon, Mary came over to me and asked what my plans were. I had decided to call myself Ralph Conway, so I told her that, and my intention to explore the world. She said that she had more or less guessed something like that from observing my tent and other gear on the bike, and the items I was carrying. She asked if I wanted a job with them and my answer was "Yes".

"Well, its not up to me of course but I will mention it to Mr Jennings and he may have a word with you."

A short while afterwards a very business-like gent, with his shirt sleeves rolled up and looking every bit "the Boss", came across and stood looking at me for a while, before saying, "I understand you are Ralph Conway and you are wishing to join my fair? Well, I can always do with a willing worker," he said, "and I would add that you seem very young to be roaming the country looking for work. But I am not going to question your private circumstances, so if you want to join us you can."

I replied that I was pleased to accept his offer.

"Right, join me on the dodgem track in five minutes or so and I will give you an introduction to our company. By the way, do you drive?" I replied that I did indeed, but had no driving licence. He said that would be no bother and he might have a driving job for me later on, away from public roads. "Come on over and join me when you are ready."

Mary met me when I went over to the fairground, and told me to

19

leave my gear behind their caravan. "You can pitch your tent there and be independent of our company." When I joined the Boss he blew his whistle loudly. Within minutes quite an assortment of workers mustered around us. "This is Ralph Conway and he is joining us from now, please accept him among us and encourage him with the benefit of your welcome and experience. Thank you, that is all!" With that he dismissed the assembly and turned to me. "I'll pay you a couple of pounds a week. It's not much but you will find you can boost it as you get to learn more of how the wheels turn in this pastime. Now, I'll leave you for a few days to just wander around, get to know the stall holders and ask any questions you wish. They will enlighten you."

At 7pm that night everything was in place and the organ was belting out popular songs, the public were coming in and within a short while the fun of the fair was in full swing. I just wandered around trying to understand as much as I could until midnight, when the fairground emptied, the lights were switched off, and I could retire to my tent and turn in. By then I was ready for sleep. Most of the day before had been riding my bike and today had been long, but it was encouraging that I had obtained a job and meant to take each day as it came. I penned a postcard to my parents, telling them I was alright and that I was working in a fair and would contact them again in the future to assure them of my progress.

Each day I learned something different. The rifle stalls were really great, as were the hoopla, darts and coconut shies. I also found the huge "Foden" traction engine fascinating, all shiny brass fittings and finely painted woodwork. It seemed to run continuously, coupled to a generator which produced electricity for all the lights and appliances.

A couple of days on the Boss asked me to go with him and take a trial driving lesson on an old and ugly USA lorry which had a large water tank mounted behind the driver's cab. This was 1933 and the truck was typical of the thirties era. Straight up and down steering column mounting a large wheel, a gate-change gear box and solid rubber tyres.

"Right Ralph, let's see if you can handle this machine," said the Boss. After an hour or two I got the hang of it, making a few trips to a water supply tank sited on the far side of the field. The Boss told me he wanted me to work with Joe Ellison, the driver of the traction engine, "and help him tend to its efficient running. It's his full-time job and he needs a good helper. Take a few days to get acquainted with Joe, who will tell you exactly what needs doing and how you should do it."

Joe was a surly character who kept himself very much to himself and his beloved engine. I soon got into a working partnership with Joe. My main job was to drive the USA to any nearby water supply and keep the water tank full. Then to transfer water to the Foden as required to run it. I also helped Joe with coal as required, feeding the firebox which heated the water which produced the steam, and so forth. Joe and I were soon a reliable team.

The weather that April–August period of summer was typical with sunny days and cold, humid evenings Most nights after the crowds had dispersed to their homes we would gather around a camp fire and swap yarns, or maybe one or more among this gifted party might bring forth violins, or an accordion and a singsong would begin. Often the women would produce a large pot of soup and sandwiches. Afterward some of us would sit in the empty 'dodgem' cars and doze away what was left of the night. As dawn approached, everyone would be up and about that day's business. We travelled from place to place around the Devizes district to which town the fair came twice yearly.

Jack Jennings, our Boss, had a brother called Jim who also owned a fair, and on rare occasions the two would meet up at the same venue and join together as one large fair. We would stop at each place for perhaps a week or 10 days at a time. On the last day, opening time was as usual in the evening, and when the punters had departed and the ground was clear everyone dismantled their respective stalls and rides and stowed them on trailers, the work continuing through the night. With big attractions like the 'chair-o-planes', 'dodgems', and so on, the roofs were dismantled first, then the side supports, followed by the base. The heaviest job of all was dismantling the sheet steel 'dodgem' flooring, which consisted of 50 × 4′×5′ wooden frames on which the steel flooring was fixed. A flat-topped lorry pulled up alongside and all the men worked together to load it in the numbered order which, unloaded at its destination, it would be put together again. As each lorry, flat-top, trailer or car was ready, off it went to join the others parked in a half-circle at the exit gate, the Boss's vehicle at the head. With dawn arriving, the column set off through the streets and into the lovely Somerset countryside. My place was in the Foden traction engine with Joe in charge and me perched in a seat over the nearside wheel, behind the small, iron steering wheel. From the steering wheel a length of heavy chain was looped, and connected to each front wheel so that by a process of steering one way the chain would pull the front wheels the other way.

It was a slow process, speed being no more than 12 mph. On top of that we also pulled the dodgems plate lorry, which was a heavy load. Behind that was the three-floor 'dodgem' trailer. At least two fairground roustabouts travelled with the trailers ready to leap off and place chocks under the wheels when we struggled uphill. The distance between sites was within a 15 mile radius, and the long line of caravans and vehicles was a familiar sight on Dorset's roads.

Individual stall-holders would often go on ahead to begin erecting their own stalls, so that when the big stuff arrived they were free to give a hand with the unloading and setting up of the main attractions. It really was a joint effort. In those balmy days in the 1930s there was little traffic on Britain's roads, so our journeying's were pleasant in the summer weather, which constituted the season, invariably hot and sunny as in 2003. I well remember being perched

22

on the Foden operating the steering wheel while Joe kept the boiler fire coaled up and the knobs and valves adjusted so that there were no problems which might impede our slow progress, plodding along the country roads lined with apple and pear orchards. Unscrupulous passers-by might be tempted by the fruit-laden trees, and we had a few of these amongst our number as was seen on numerous occasions. If I glanced in the rear-view mirror I could see lads drop off trucks and leap over walls and hedges into the orchards. Sometimes this delicious English fruit would be distributed up the line to the drivers and cab crews.

It would be about mid to late afternoon when we arrived at our destination, where sites would be picked for the shows and unloading would begin. The lorries would be parked and after a break for tea and a light lunch of soup or sandwiches, everyone would begin work and continue long into the night. Then it was up early next morning and complete the job of assembling before midday, when we would set out for the town shops to get fish and chips or whatever else was available. Opening time for the fair would be 6pm, or earlier if there were customers about. After a week we would be on our way again, and so life continued as we dealt each day with whatever came along. New faces would appear and old ones would leave. There were no goodbyes or 'cards' to collect, no questions asked. Most fairs moved to Olympia in London at the end of the season, where they could remain under cover and perform through the winter months until it was time to begin the cycle once again.

I had joined Jack Jennings Fair back in May 1933 when I was 13 years old, and it was towards the middle of August that I began to realise that I would soon have to decide what my next move would be. It certainly was not going to involve working at Olympia. My itchy feet wanted to be on the move again, and the ideal solution manifested itself one evening after we had returned to Devizes at the end of a particularly busy Saturday night.

Several of us were sitting in dodgems, having a break and a chat when a ginger haired chap came over and sat in the car next to mine and asked what my future plans were.

"You aren't going to Olympia, are you?" he said? I replied that I had yet to make up my mind. He then asked "Why don't you join me on a different exercise Ralph. I'm going to leave next Saturday night. The fair is off to London on the Sunday. What say we get a couple of days bed & breakfast and you can sell your bike and tent, after which we can set off for Liverpool, find a ship and work our passage to Canada and see what is on offer over there?"

He was 22 years old and his suggestion suited me fine, so I agreed, asking how we would get to Liverpool!

"We can walk and take our own time, getting an odd job here, another there and move on as we feel like it." I liked the idea of setting off on the road again, but wasn't sure about Canada, but agreed to go along with 'Ginger'. We got ourselves accommodation in Devizes and sold our belongings next day. After a meal, and on approaching our 'digs' we saw a police van parked outside, which did not concern us until we went inside and were approached by two uniformed constables. They asked us to accompany them to the police station "to answer a few questions." To our knowledge we had committed no crime, but looking back I could see how the landlady might have become suspicious about my age, and then when our excess baggage and cycle disappeared she must have wondered. She had obviously become concerned and telephoned the local police station, to which we were now heading, along with our suitcases into which we had packed what was left of our possessions.

We were placed in different rooms, and when we were alone the Sergeant asked me my name.

"Ralph Conway", I replied. "I have been working with 'Ginger' on Jack Jenning's fair, which has now gone to London for the winter. We didn't want to go with them and so we are making our way to

Liverpool and have the aim of working our passage to Canada to find work there."

"What a load of old rubbish," said the Sergeant. "We know all about you. You are Ron Walsh of Lymington, and your parents requested that we inform them if you appeared in this area. Do you confirm that you are Ron Walsh? That being so we will inform your parents that we are sending you back home."

I confirmed my name, but told him that I was not ready to go home yet, and if sent back I would push off again. He said he would see what my parents had to say and what they wanted him to do. I was taken with 'Ginger' for the Inspector to deal with. The Inspector had already telephoned my parents by then, and they had allowed me the freedom to continue with my 'hairbrained' scheme, "but when it falls through you are to be put on a train and sent home." He also added that the police would be watching out for us all the way along our route.

Next morning we were off northwards, walking all day until we arrived at what became our favourite 'kip-down', a straw-filled roofed barn with no sides. It was ideal, and now that the evening was upon us we climbed on top for the night. These stacks were to be found all along our route, and we would climb into a convenient, lofty perch each night and, fully rested and refreshed, would up at the crack of dawn walking mile after monotonous mile, picking blackberries when we came upon any, for our supper.

At first our aiming point was Birmingham, where we tried to get jobs in the Austin car factory but were unsuccessful in adding to our shrinking finances, so we continued northwards. It was customary to fence off road-works in those days and a watchman in a little wooden shelter would be installed to look after them so that no one fell in. He would always have a brazier on the go during his lonely nightshift, so when we saw a glow ahead we could be assured of a warm welcome and a couple of hours chat with a brew thrown in.

One evening about a week into our journey, at about 10pm we went through a small town, and as we left through the outskirts we came across just such a watchman. As we sat there at 11pm a crowd of people approached, obviously a wedding party from their jollity. They joined us at the fire, still in their best bib and tucker of wedding suits and dresses. For an hour or so we all sang songs and got talking. The leader of the group was more than slightly interested in us two, and he told us of a small-holding just along the road where he kept a number of donkeys, chickens, and geese, and he offered us a few days board in exchange for helping him build new chicken runs, digging some ditches, and a few other jobs. He would also pay us a few pounds to help us on our way. Back we went with him where he showed us a newly erected run and shed where we could live during our short stay. It was primitive but adequate!

We were there for a week and then it was back on the road and a lot of miles through uninteresting countryside where there were fewer haystacks and so, if we came upon an empty building or shed, we would sleep there overnight. By this time we were both showing a marked lack of interest in either Liverpool or Canada, as we grew wearier and wearier. Or should I say this applied more to me, for my pal seemed unaffected by it all, though both of us could do with a good bath by then. We managed to get a bath at a cafe outside Ironbridge, along with a hot meal. My feet were heavily blistered and causing me some concern, and they were steadily getting worse the more I walked and slowing me up, which didn't please 'Ginger'. He began to forge ahead and decided that I had become a liability, and eventually the time came when he failed to stop and wait for me, or come back, but walked on and I never saw him again.

Alone now I managed to find a police station, told them my story, and was soon on a train back to Devizes where I was met by a policeman and taken to the station. After a wonderful welcome they all wanted to know how I had got on. I was looked after very well until they put me on a train to Lymington accompanied by a constable, who came all the way with me. My father was awaiting when the train pulled in, having been advised of the return of the prodigal son. He thanked my escort and I was soon back at home among my family.

A few days later I told Dad that I would go to the Royal Hospital School as he had suggested, and then into the Royal Navy, provided I passed the necessary entrance examinations, of course. The school was for boys, and boarded the sons of ex- or serving Royal Marines or Royal Navy personnel. Two weeks later, after my father had sent to Greenwich for the entrance forms. I went with him to London, and passed the medical in the morning and educational exam in the afternoon.

In August 1933 when I was just 13 years and 8 months old, joined the school at Holbrook near Ipswich.

Chapter 3

I JOIN THE MERCHANT NAVY

When I volunteered to enter The Royal Hospital School I understood that it was attached to Greenwich College in London where sons of former members of the Royal Navy were admitted from as young as 11 years old to be trained in naval matters as well as ordinary academic subjects, as boarding members until reaching the age of about 16 years. At that age they then entered the Royal Navy as Boy's 2nd Class. For ever after they would be known as "Greenwich Schoolboys."

I arrived at Greenwich following my call-up in August 1933 and found that things had changed considerably. A new establishment had been built in the countryside, at Holbrook near Ipswich, Suffolk, and we new lads were to be taken there in a day or so. It was now called the Royal Hospital School, and was a splendid set of buildings set in acres of grass playing fields, sloping down to a river which curled along its bottom boundary. An impressive clock tower rose from the centre of a long colonnade of school rooms and offices, above which were classrooms and also the headmaster's study. During my time there the head was a Mr. Sheldrake. In front of the colonnade was a large tarmac parade ground with, on the far side, a tall fully-rigged mast, and set around its base a safety net. Behind this was an underground firing range which was manned by Chief Petty Officer Cooper.

A large number of living quarters were built around the parade ground, each block being able to accommodate about 40 ratings. These were further divided into Junior Blocks and Senior Blocks, all named after famous naval heroes. I went into Nelson Block as did everyone joining the R.H.S. After a month of settling in as new arrivals we were moved from Nelson into our first proper block – New Entry – from where we would go to a senior block, which would become our permanent quarters for the rest of our time there. Each house was run by a resident 'Housemaster' and a Nursing Sister.

Blocks had the master's accommodation on the ground floor, where the recreational, rest, study rooms, and toilets could also be found. On the floor above there was a dormitory to one side, which ran the whole length of the building, and this contained, on the opposite side of the floor, showers and toilets. These two places were served by a passageway from the centre of the shower room to the centre of the dormitory, an area used by the Housemaster for nightly prayers or the administering of punishments.

Day to day routine was much the same between seasonal holidays, which were two weeks at Christmas, Easter and Summer. These were the only times we were allowed out of the school boundaries. Each day began with jumping out of bed at 6.30am and removing our flannel nightshirts, which reached to just below the knees, then to run naked along the passageway to stand under the showers, at which time the master would turn on the cold water. Evening showers were usually hot. We dried ourselves then ran back to the dormitory, where we stood by our beds until told to dress and proceed to breakfast in the main dining hall across the parade ground. The whole school would stand to attention at the dining tables until Mr. Lumsden blew his whistle for silence and the Head would say prayers, after which another blast signalled that we could sit and eat. This routine was the same every morning, noon, and night!

Everything we did was well planned, from sport to leisure occupations, education to activities, and worked as well as a brand new machine of many parts. On weekdays we wore a blue jersey, black shorts, long stockings and black shoes. Two coloured rings ran around the stocking turndowns, and these indicated the house of the wearer. In my case, red for 'Cornwallis' (Junior) and later 'Blake' (Senior). 'Hawke' and 'St. Vincent' were white, 'Raleigh' and 'Drake', blue. On Sundays, parades and special days, and when we went on long leave, we wore our Naval uniform. The day before a long leave was special and looked forward to eagerly. It was known as 'Leave Cash Day' for obvious reasons, and was a day free of official activities.

After leave it was back to normal routine, which would include schooling, seamanship, mast-climbing, sports sessions, rifle range and so forth. Discipline was intense, and anyone caught smoking or defaulting was awarded strokes of the cane, which were administered to one's rear with enthusiasm. 'Cuts', as they were called, were made by the Housemaster to those who defaulted in his house out of school hours. Otherwise it was left to the Schoolmaster to deal with all other 'school-hours' punishments. For serious sexual deviancy, the Captain would deal with the punishment. Such serious punishments were carried out in a service-like manner in the gymnasium, with the cuts being awarded. The offender would be brought to the gym at around a quarter to noon, and as the clock struck the time so the cane was given to its stroke. A number of witnesses were always required to be present, including the Captain himself, a Medical Officer, Master-at-Arms and whosoever was designated. These serious punishments were rare but the minor ones were fairly frequent. I had the misfortune to collect two 'awards', one from the Housemaster and the other from the Schoolmaster.

It was after returning from a summer leave period that I decided to try out my new pea-shooter. One slack afternoon I had collected some Hawthorn berries from the trees, which grew at the bottom of the sports field. Aimlessly potting at various pillars on the opposite side of an empty muster area in 'Blakes' precinct, I was not aware that the House Nursing Sister had appeared until she screamed as a berry hit her in the neck. I was called over and she confiscated the evidence and informed me that I should find Housemaster Mr.

Dowell at 6pm in his office where I could explain my actions. My excuses were not considered acceptable, so at bed time muster in the dormitory I would receive cuts of the cane.

The routine for bed never varied through the year, with assembly at 7.30pm in the dorm after supper, to stand by our beds and wait for the appearance of the Housemaster, who would tell us to undress completely and make our way to the showers, where we would stand and wait again until he came to turn on the water. His mood could usually be gauged by whether he allowed us cold or hot water. Five minutes later we would dry ourselves quickly, run back to our beds, don the nightshirts and wait for prayers and permission to turn in. Mr. Dowell was very athletic, slim, 40 years old, and stood at 6 feet 2 inches. He was an extremely competent golfer and well suited to using the cane. Now that prayers were over I was required to put on a pair of short trousers under my nightshirt and then stand in the square in the middle of the dorm whilst every one else stood to attention alongside their beds. The Housemaster conducted the punishment by standing next to me, cane in hand, whereupon I was instructed to bend over and touch my toes. The cane was aligned with my rear end, and after a couple of test swings came the delivery of the first stroke. It was always the same. The boy would jerk upright as the body and mind reacted in total surprise to the immediate pain of that first stroke. He was allowed to rub the offended part and the master would then push him back to the bent position by placing the cane on his shoulder, and then would come 'cut' number two, etc. With my three 'cuts' completed I was told to return to my bed and ordered to turn in. Next morning, and for a few after that, three bruises clearly showed themselves during shower periods.

My second and final punishment took place some months later after a classroom incident. All masters wore a gown and mortarboard. This particular Thursday afternoon 'Schooly' had been prattling on about some historical affair and, for whatever reason, I had lost interest and was doodling in a scrapbook, making a cartoon likeness of his face although with an enlarged nose. I was just drawing in his mortar-board at a rakish angle when from behind me he made his presence known. Obviously, not appreciating my artistic efforts he simply said "get the punishment book and cane." Off I went to the Head study and knocked on the door, from behind which "Come" issued forth, and I went in and approached Mr. Sheldrake. I told him what I had come for, upon which he asked me to take my pick of the canes in the large wall cabinet. There were so many it was difficult to know, as each could do damage of a different kind. The thick one would leave a wide blue line, the thin one a possible cut, so I chose a medium one. Back in class there was immediate action. The incident was written up in the book and three stripes were imprinted onto my backside. I returned the book and cane to the Head and that was that!

The most common reason for punishment was smoking, and although I indulged with the rest I was never caught or punished again for any reason. It was beyond me why most of those caught puffing away at those sinful weed sticks, strictly forbidden, did so in the large block of heads under the parade ground terrace, for it was an obvious place for a duty agent to look. I, and a couple of 'oppos', thought we had the answer to a few illicit drags, and that was to shin up the mast when it was dark and sit on the first, wide, platform. Provided we cupped our hands over the glowing end of the cigarette it could not be seen, and the smoke disappeared into the night sky. We could see all around of course so we didn't get caught and puffed away to our hearts content. If anything was forbidden everyone would try it. In reality it was a daft place to be and should have been at the top of any patrol's list, but our luck always held.

The months passed in strict routine, our minds fully occupied. When I was about 15 plus a few months, I was informed that I was going to *H.M.S. Ganges* at nearby Shotley to pass exams to enter the Navy as a Boy 2nd Class. It was a fairly full day for all those taking the Educational Exams in the morning and having a full Medical in the afternoon, and there was a shock to come for, as we were lined up naked in Sick Bay, the doctor, who had slowly passed down the line studying our fine physiques stopped in front of me, moved on then came back.

"How long have you had those?", indicating my feet.
"Since I was born, Sir."
"No, no, I mean those bunions."
"I didn't know I had any, Sir."
"Well, you have and although they are hardly visible now they will grow and could cause you problems in the future." The Medical Officer, I learnt on return to school, failed me for the Royal Navy. During the following two weeks I was interviewed by the Resettlement Officer to sort out my next move. I would not be discharged into 'civvie street' until I had a position to go to. My choice was a job in the catering industry in a London hotel, in the motor trade, or as a deck boy in the Merchant Service, and that was my first choice. If I were based in Southampton it was close to home in Lymington.

A few days later I was informed that I had a job as a deck boy with the Union Castle Line at Southampton, and was to join the RMS *Warwick Castle*, a large liner, which sailed between Southampton and South Africa. Ten days were spent in Southampton and then she sailed to Madeira, Capetown, where she stayed for a few days, then up the East Coast of Africa to Port Elizabeth, East London, Durban, where she picked up more passengers for the UK, then back up the West Coast to Madeira again before sailing to Southampton and starting the whole thing over again.

The long days at sea were never boring, just the opposite in fact, especially for an adventurous young man. The days were hot and lazy, with passengers lounging on deck, and we lads scurrying about the decks doing the many jobs which were ours alone. We ten 'Deck Boys' had our own mess and living quarters, and were in the charge of a couple of senior hands who saw to our instruction. Daily routine was straightforward including, in the forenoon, washing decks, taking care that any early rising passengers were not inconvenienced, and then it was on to one of our main jobs of ditching the main galley waste. Beside each galley was a large area where all waste materials were tossed. These could include wooden boxes, sacks of vegetable peelings, general waste and large square tins with a big round hole in the top. These had held coffee or tea. The lids generally had been discarded when we got to them, and were usually part filled with coloured liquid, the residue their contents. One of these tins played the central part in an incident during my third trip, which almost cost me my life, but I will return to that a bit later on.

After dinner we generally relaxed in the heat, being allowed to do as we pleased within the rules. Some slept the hours away, but most of us would gather on the forecastle deck watching over the guard rail at the vast expanse of shimmering sea. First of all there appeared to be little of interest, but as we watched the entertainment would surely unfold, as it did on my third trip. Suddenly a giant ray leapt from the sea and returned with a huge splash. Shoals of flying fish would suddenly appear and fly for a long distance. They made frequent appearances, and occasionally some came aboard to land struggling on the decks. Usually we threw these back to the sea. Our favourite thing was to lean out over the guard rail and look straight down some 20 feet or so to the surface, where sharks and porpoise swam along with the ship, brushing against its moving sides and then rolling over and over or leaping out of the water. A favourite pastime was to see someone lean out shaking a loaf of bread at them – the sharks would become very agitated, and when the loaf was let go one would invariably leap and roll into the air and grab it before falling back with a splash into its natural element.

The sharks often kept close to the ship's stern waiting for the rubbish we boys threw overboard, especially during the early forenoon when we did our clearing up. The one odd shark would suddenly become a large frenzied pack as they all homed in on the 'gash'. We all thought it was great fun (on reflection it was a silly and unkind pastime born of fear) to aim our boxes and cartons right at the sharks to see if we could hit one.

One morning we were collecting 'gash' from outside the main galley and I got a large, square, empty coffee tin with its usual stained water residue sloshing around inside. As I looked to see if I could heave it over and score a direct hit, I swung it around my head before letting it go. It didn't quite go as planned, for a sharp edge of tin buried itself in my fingers and the weight of the tin as I threw it took me over the rail. My feet left the deck and as they did so two hands grabbed my ankles. The Bosun, who had been watching, had moved swiftly and saved my life. The grab I had made for the centre rail support as I went by it, plus the Bosun's quick thinking meant I lived to learn a lesson. Blood dripped down to the water from my fingers and the waiting sharks may have thought that a good meal was on its way, but there would be no fresh meat that day. The tin was eased off my fingers and it fell away into the sea. The sick berth attendant did his first-aid and I was put on light duties. On my return to full duty I had little interest anymore in where the rubbish landed when I tossed it overboard.

A deck boy's job in the Merchant Navy was a good one, and the weather was almost always sunny, with hot seas, and mostly it was also calm on that South African run. Work was straightforward and time off ample. Well known celebrities were often to be found amongst the passengers, and most were not above chatting to us. Many of them were film actors and actresses. One celebrity was a boxer known as 'Kid Berg' (late 1935), who was on his way to fight in Cape Town. Once alongside in South Africa we were allowed ashore, and were expected to behave properly with the company reputation in mind. We could enjoy ourselves as long as we were back on board in good time. Organised free trips were laid on for the crew at various ports of call, and the National Safari Park is one which is imprinted on my memory. We left the ship's side at 9am and travelled to the park which was near Durban, and stayed in the coach all the time except for a couple of meal breaks. All the animals of Africa could be seen close to as we passed through their territory.

I was almost 16 years old, and these trips began to pall a bit, seeing and doing the same things trip after trip, and as we sailed on the homeward leg once again I vowed to do something about it when we got back. The routine on arrival at Southampton, usually at about 9.30–10 am, was to have one's cases packed and ready to leave the ship for the 10 day break. We would file past a desk in one of the shore-side offices near the gangway and sign ourselves off. If we wanted to do the next seven week trip we were required to be at the office at the stated date and sign on again. If we didn't turn up, we were no longer part of the crew!

On my way from the docks to the Hants and Dorset bus station near the Civic Centre, I passed the Royal Navy Recruiting Office, but this time instead of going on by I entered and asked to join up. My particulars were taken, and when they said they would be in touch I didn't realise it would be within a week. At the office I had a medical and educational exam, passing both, and signed on as a Boy 2nd Class. I returned home to await call-up, which was delivered by post a few days later, telling me to go to *H.M.S. Wildfire* at Sheerness, Kent.

So began the next chapter in my eventful life, which was filled for the next 33 years by service in the Royal Navy.

Chapter 4

H.M.S. FOYLEBANK

I had been on board two naval ships, deserting from one due to inflexible rules, worked for a travelling fair, been to Naval College, sailed to Africa several times in the Merchant Navy, sold meat products for a butchery firm, and been lucky re-joining the navy in having a far sighted and fair Commodore undertake my post desertion trial.

Now I was off to war. I was 'kitted up', given a Mess, and as a trained seaman joined the 'boys' waiting for a draft in the Royal Naval Barracks at Portsmouth, to wherever fate and the Movements Officer wanted me. A new ship was being commissioned, and a lot of draft chits were appearing in the messes. One of them was for me, so I did not have long to wait. I and several others were to be part of the crew of *H.M.S. Foylebank*. Just three weeks after returning to the RN, a newly redeemed one-time deserter, I was back in the picture and in the war wondering what lay ahead.

The day came when all of us drafted to the *Foylebank* were mustered at a railway siding inside H.M.S. Victory Barracks. We lugged our bags and hammocks, stowing them in a guard's van, sorted out our seats and settled down for the long journey to Belfast shipyard via Stranraer in Scotland. Whilst the ship was fitting out we were allocated our messes on board, and gradually settled in. Originally *Foylebank* was one of the 'Bank Line' of merchant ships, which the navy had taken over for conversion into quite formidable Anti-Aircraft (Ack-Ack) ships. Several of these ships were converted for Harbour Defence, and sited at various strategic ports around the country, where they would act as permanent gun platforms until enough shoreside batteries could be constructed. Others in the line were *Allanbank* and *Ladybank*, and each was transformed into a Royal Navy warship with mountings of four twin 3 inch 'ack-ack' guns (A.B.X.Y. Mountings), the A & B being forrard and X&Y down aft. Amidships were port and starboard mountings of multiple 'pom-poms', and port and starboard 0.5 multiple machine guns, which amounted to a formidable array of weaponry to deter any attacking aircraft. Also installed was a Type 280 Radar which was very efficient when it came to all round detection of possible enemy aircraft.

One difference in the manning of *Foylebank* that was most outstanding was that we carried no RN engine-room staff at all. We had retained all the original Merchant Navy stokers (greasers as they were called in the civilian service) and they all came under the designation of T124 personnel. The Engineer Officers were also from the original crew. I think that this had been planned because almost all of our time would either be spent at anchor or anchored at whatever strategic in-harbour site we were designated to go to.

After acceptance and sea trials, which were all satisfactory, we proceeded to sea from Belfast. When we were sufficiently far from shore the Captain cleared lower deck and informed us that he had "opened our sealed orders". These told us that we were to proceed to Portland where we would become the Harbour Defence Ship. As we approached the harbour a mine exploded nearby, sending up a huge plume of water. Luckily we suffered no damage to ship or crew. We passed the breakwater and moored between two buoys about 400 yards from the dockyard stores and other buildings which, except for one trip to sea for a few hours work on the main engines, was where we stayed during the rest of our time there.

The day after our arrival an interesting 'pipe' was made over the ship's tannoy. "Any junior rating having a driving licence, report to the Master-at-Arms." Normally one would observe the unwritten law to "never volunteer" because, more often than not, it would turn out to be the visitation of some unwanted trouble of one sort or another. I gave this a lot of thought, and decided that it might lead to a 'cushy number', which all matelots are seeking all the time. Casting caution to the four winds, I made my way to the Regulating Office and produced my driving licence to the MAA. After a few questions as to my experience, he said "Right then Walsh, as from now you are the engineer and driver of our motor boat. It will be full-time job and you will be excused all duties except 'action-stations', and likewise, exercises. The boat will have a cox'n, bow and stern men, but you will be responsible for engine maintenance and driving the boat; are you happy with that?" I replied to the effect that it was not quite what I was expecting, but I thought I could cope. He bade me get into the boat and and make myself familiar with the engine. "The boat's crew are already there", he added "so have a few dummy runs alongside and so forth. " He also told me that our first official run was to take the postman ashore with the mail at 0930, and that the boat would wait for him to return with the incoming mail.

There were plenty of other trips that day, and the following ones, each sunset ending with the liberty men being collected at 10.30pm. There was no overnight leave, and weekends were granted only for special requests. From then on a lot of my time was spent in the motor-boat, which suited me fine at first because the engine room was enclosed, with a long seat alongside the engine and out of sight of prying eyes. We all began to settle down into our jobs and various routines with numerous 'action stations', 'cruising stations', and so on thrown in. My cruising station was in the H.A.C.P. (High Angle Control Position) situated under the ship's bridge. It was a space of about 15 feet square with a long rectangular table in the centre. All the settings and firing-order set-ups to control all eight of the high angle 3 inch guns of A.B.X. and Y. mountings were there, manned by an officer and two Leading Seamen, plus a variety of others including S.A.'s, chefs, and so forth. This was also my 'cruising station'. My 'action station' was Range Setter on the left-hand of X gun mounting at the ship's stern.

As the days passed a feeling of normality settled over the ship, with its routines established. Action stations were sounded often as German aircraft came over on reconnaissance or mine-laying missions in Weymouth Bay and around Portland Harbour. They would be seen mainly during early evening or heard at night. We would close up at our guns, our searchlights picking out the enemy. More often than not, they would be too low for the searchlights to depress, and there was the mole in between. I could be found, in between all the routines, out in the motor-boat or closed up on X gun. The Germans had several air bases around the Cherbourg area now that they had conquered France and the rest of Europe, so they were frequent visitors over England going on bombing trips or coming back from them. Our position was rather vulnerable to say the least, with France only 20 minutes flying time away.

In our free moments we would listen to 'Lord Haw Haw', the British traitor who broadcast propaganda for the Germans. His name was William Joyce, and when he was captured after the war he was tried and hanged for treason. His task, from his base in Germany, was to demoralise civilians and servicemen alike with his mixture of lies and the truth. He told the world on three occasions that they had sunk the carrier *Ark Royal*. Most British listeners soon became bored with his monotonous voice and the utter rubbish he spoke, and just turned off their radio. However, once he even mentioned our ship and the Admiralty.

On the *Foylebank* my 'cushy' little number as a driver was becoming a real bone of contention. I had managed to upset the Master-at-Arms quite a lot either by frequently requesting a relief from the job or for someone else to work with me so that I could have a run ashore sometimes like everyone else aboard the ship. There is always a price to pay for any 'good' job or everyone would want to do it, but he promised that he would see what he could do about it. One day he told me he had found the answer: "When you want a run ashore, see me and I will arrange a relief for the motor-boat." Two days later I did just that, and he sent a T124 Engineer Lieutenant who did not appear all that enthusiastic about the idea which, I guess, was understandable. As it happened I only managed two more runs ashore that way, then it was back to the old routine which I was not pleased about either. Especially so because an elder brother of mine was on a ship in Portland Harbour at the time.

D u ring one of my shore runs brother John and I went to Weymouth where we were walking when a Navy Patrol car drew up alongside, and "Are you from the *Foylebank?*" was shouted at us. He told me to get back to my ship as she was being bombed. There was obviously no point in rushing, but when we did arrive back we could see no sign of enemy activity. I bade my brother farewell and caught the next boat back to the ship, where I soon heard that earlier in the evening a German plane had carried out a high-level bombing attack supposedly on *Foylebank* but had hit Chessil Beach and the dockyard instead. There was not much damage done to any of the supposed targets apparently. Just a 'tip and run' raider testing the local defences, and probably photographing the area at the same time.

The next evening most of us were in the forrard mess deck having our supper when over the radio came the voice we had grown to hate, the familiar call sign of "Germany calling, Germany calling (only he said 'Jairmany') if the British Admiralty do not shift that ack ack ship swinging around its buoy in Portland Harbour we will send our Luftwaffe (airforce) over there and do it for them!" Lots of laughter from us and a few choice remarks, then the incident was forgotten. Life continued as normal. The following morning, at breakfast time, or thereabouts, the MAA came into the mess deck. 'Right Walsh, I have got a relief for you. You've got today and tomorrow to 'gen' him up on the boat driver's routine. Take him on your daily runs, then he will take over from you on Thursday morning first trip of the day with the postman. You, Walsh, will start off your part-of-ship duties by being cook of the mess. "I put my relief right and he soon got the hang of the job.

The 3rd July (1940), evening, the last run of the day had taken

IN THE COMPANY OF HEROES

place and I said to my 'oppo' , "OK, then it is all yours now, your first trip will be taking the 'Posty' ashore at 9am so you had best be down at the boat straight after your breakfast, then you are clear of the mess, and take a paper or book with you to read until the boat is called away."

The 4th July started off like any other day, it was lovely and bright and I was with my chum on the forward mess deck. He was on the same gun (X) as myself. We had finished scrubbing out and the mess looked immaculate with all the hammocks stowed away in their nettings, just as they would be in Nelson's time. Up on deck there had apparently been a great deal of activity as rumours of aeroplanes being sighted heading towards Portland buzzed around between the crew. Of course, down below we only knew what people wanted to tell us until, from the tannoy there came that clamouring sound "Action Stations", and I shouted to my chum "Let's get up there then". We sped out into the racket of gunfire and loud bangs, and made for our gun station. As I stepped over the door combing there came a terrific explosion from behind, and I was blown clean out of the door and across the canteen flat on my stomach. I hauled myself upright and went back into the mess where an appaling sight met me. From the back of the mess door I could see wooden mess tables on fire, their metal legs twisted into strange shapes. Hammocks were fiercely blazing, burning through the netting. With others I began to make my way down the port side below decks, towards the stern, and as I did so there was either a near miss from a bomb or a direct hit, I didn't know which. The ship appeared to lift out of the water, shudder, then drop back again with a thud. We all had got about half-way along the port side when, from the engine room, came another terrific explosion. The ship's side blew out, and from our position we could see the dockyard through the gaping hole. The deck head was severely split as well so we had to turn back and make our way along the starboard side.

Halfway along there appeared a big shaft of sunlight shining down the ladder through the upper deck hatch, from where the sound of

H.M.S. Foylebank on fire during the bombing attack on 4th July 1940

voices shouting orders filtered through into the hell below. Then astern of me machine-gun bullets splattered down the hatch. As soon as it was clear to do so we got past and into the sickbay flat where a lot of the non-combatants had gathered including T124 ratings and RN writers, SBA's, etc. The SBA's had begun to tend wounded men.

I made my way through the huddled mass of men and began to climb the iron bulkhead ladder to the shell handling room, and then on up further to the X gun mounting platform. I had hesitated in the shell room because it was a small, enclosed space, pitch dark, and it was difficult to breathe with the heat and dust. There was some sunlight streaming down but that just lit up where it fell. The atmosphere was now full of floating particles shaken free by the explosions and I had to get into fresh air or choke. Finally, I made it into the glare of that summer morning's sunshine and as I expected, saw none of the gun crew where they would have been, and surmised that they must be dead or wounded as they tried to close up to their gun. I clearly recall now my reaction as I stood there on that empty gun deck alone, after coming from the dark hell down below, with German dive bombers screaming over us at mast height fulfilling Lord Haw Haw's prophesy as they also machine gunned our upper deck. I must have cut an odd sight standing on that gun deck alone, about 15 feet above the upper deck, in my blue overalls, one shoe missing, face black with white stripes. The blast, I found out later, had rolled whole strips of skin up my face and the white stripes were what was underneath, the black being my original top layer of skin dirtied by blast. A bomb came flying past the upper structure of X gun mounting, through the upper deck steel plate and exploded in the sick bay among those 20 poor guys seeking shelter. They would have known nothing about it when they died. Looking down onto the upper deck brought home to me then what this was all about. My mind took in huge swathes of information, the huge holes where bombs had crashed through steel decks, each gap with smoke and fire pouring out. Twisted metal was sculpted among shattered upper deck fittings. Amidst it all were the shattered and broken bodies of men I knew well, the victims of blast, flying metal, machine gun bullets, all lying on top of one another in heaps as more bombers roared over, taking their time to make sure the ship and crew, obviously already dying, were well and truly smashed. I kept thinking to myself, why were we not closed up and ready for them? Why were we allowed to be taken by surprise? Had we been alert we could have given a very different account of ourselves. We had the most modern radar!

As the hell continued other boats, smaller ones like the tug *Sundial* which was towing two barges at the time the enemy struck. One 'Stuka' machine gunned the small group and dropped a stick of bombs, one of which went down the funnel of the tug and another alongside the barge that carried a sailor called Stan Whetlor who had been watching the terrible attack on *Foylebank*. Stan was one of four men picked up from the water by rescue boats seeking survivors from among other small boats among the mayhem.

Someone behind me was shouting orders in very nautical language and I peered over the mounting boundary wall onto 'Y' gun mounting, the coconut splinter matting surrounding it ablaze. A couple of the gun crew were frantically running around as the gun captain barked orders in rapid succession. He was Leading Seaman "Badger Otley' who was demanding his men bring him shell to ram up the breech of his gun. Looking up I saw a Ju87 (Stuka) coming straight down at us and 'Badger' wanted to deal with it in his service-like manner. "Give, me some bloody ammo," he screamed above the din. They called back that "There's only these practice shells in the ready racks." "Well, what are you waiting for?", he yelled, "give me those."

By this time the main attack had eased off and we were listing to port with a huge cloud of thick black smoke rising into the sky from our stern. Someone on the upper deck was shouting, "Anyone on X gun?" I went to the side and looked over to see the First Lieutenant, who asked me if anyone was alive up there. "Only me" I said. "Well get yourself down here and make your way forrard – we will be abandoning ship very shortly."

There was only one way for me to go and that was over the guard rail and down the iron ladder, welded to the bulkhead, to get to the upper deck 15 feet below. I soon discovered that only five feet of the ladder remained, the rest having been blown away, so I dropped the last few feet. Unluckily I landed on my back onto a kedge anchor, which was secured into position on the deck, and that is how I suffered my only bad injury in that mayhem. I didn't have time to give it a second thought as so much was still happening.

Making my way towards the bows I had reached amidships, where the passageway between the engine room bulkhead and the starboard guard rail had been reduced to about eight feet in width, and there I stopped, for there was a pile of bodies in the way. "Push your way through them, or walk over them, they are all dead" said Petty Officer Sansome the Gunnery P.O. who was standing in the

H.M.S. Foylebank during attack, 4 July 1940, on fire amidships half an hour before 'Abandon Ship!'

gangway just before the starboard 'pompom' mounting. As I came up to him I saw there were four others waiting and he told me to "stay with them, Mantle hasn't finished yet, when he has we will need to get him down and over the side into one of those boats ". Apparently a bomb had exploded near Leading Seaman Jack Mantle's gun and killed and injured his gun - crew and he himself had a shattered left leg but had dragged himself up to the gun and prepared to engage the enemy. This one had dropped the bomb and was even now ready to attack again with machine guns having turned over the Mole and headed back towards us. Jack Mantle, although in great pain had the five barrels of his pom poms trained on the incoming enemy. The Leading Seaman was struggling to pull back the 'change-over' lever on top of the gun from 'Electrics' to 'Hand-Firing'. It had been slightly bent by blast and he was cursing as the range closed, then, in the last few seconds the enemy gunner and Mantle opened fire together. I was uncertain as to what happened in the next few seconds. Had the plane gone by or exploded into pieces? Mantle was slumped over his gun either due to his former wounds or due to the Stuka's machine-gun fire I can't say. What I am sure of is that Leading Seaman Mantle was still alive then. Now it was a case of rescuing the survivors, many of them badly injured, and get them off the ship before it went down.

We got Jack Mantle and his crew off the gun mounting and lowered them one by one into small boats which had been standing off during the action and dodging enemy machine-guns, but had now come alongside to our assistance. All their crews showed immense courage by being so near where the bombs, machine guns, and shrapnel could have got them. Some had been injured, some had boats sunk under them, there had been near misses, as we heard later.

Those of us left on *Foylebank* and still able, were split into two search parties and sent below, led by the 'Jimmy'. We found no one alive down there in the rapidly filling hull so we returned to the outside to further assist the work being carried out on the upper deck. Having done all we could we made our way wearily, up to the focsle and lowered ourselves over the bows onto a couple of large tenders which waited to take us to shore at Boscawen, part of the dockyard. There we were treated for minor cuts and bruises and the hospital cases were taken to Portland Hospital close by. A rudimentary role call during which our mail was brought to us showed that a majority of names were not being answered. It was not until that afternoon, about 2pm, several coaches arrived to take us to the Royal Naval Barracks at Portsmouth. Within four days we received new kit and were sent home on 14 days survivors leave.

An official list of Officers and men serving on *H.M.S.Foylebank*, at the time of the attack on 4th July 1940 states that from a total of 292 Officers and Men aboard *H.M.S.Foylebank* a total of 72 people lost their lives, including 14 Officers from an original number of 28. For his actions during the attack, Leading Seaman Jack Mantle was, on 3rd September 1940, awarded a posthumous Victoria Cross, Britain's highest award for gallantry. His citation reads:

Leading Seaman Jack Mantle was in charge of the Starboard Pom Pom when H.M.S.Foylebank was attacked by enemy aircraft on 4th July 1940. Early in the action his left leg was shattered by a bomb, but he stood fast to his gun and went on firing with hand gear only, for the ships electric power had failed. Almost at once he was wounded again in many places. Between his bursts of fire he had no time to reflect on the grievous injuries of which he was soon to die, but his great courage bore him up to the end of the fight when he fell by the gun he had so valiantly served.

An official report of the action read as follows:

"On the morning of 3rd July 1940 'Jerry' made a further reconnaissance trip taking photographs of Foylebank lying in harbour. The next morning, on July 4th 1940, the sun rose into a cloudless sky and whilst men went about their

Jack Mantle's grave in R.N. Cemetry Portland

duties, signals were being received that 'Jerry' was in the area. It was, and had become, the sort of situation that the men aboard had become acquainted with since arrival in the area. At exactly 0840 hrs 'Jerry' was overhead with 26 Ju87 'Stuka' dive bombers.of the type first seen. used in Spain, and then again as they blasted the armies of Europe into submission, which proceeded to fall screaming from the sky to loose their deadly load on to the ship and its crew. They came at us in formations of 3 & 5 for the next 8 minutes and Foylebanks guns, those that their crews had been able to man, fought back ferociously. With 22 direct hits her electrics out of action, guns not damaged or destroyed with enough men available, had to be fired by hand.

Some time after the war, in April 1969, when I had retired from the Royal Navy and was working at *H.MS.Collingwood*. Fareham, as a civilian transport driver, I learned that a fellow survivor was attempting to trace survivors of our old ship with a view to starting up an annual *Foylebank* Re-Union to be held on or around the anniversary of 4th July. Peter Davies, from Cheshire, who had been one of Jack Mantles gun crew and was badly wounded early on in the action was the man in question.

Around 55 of us answered the copious advertising which Peter had put out in various media all over the UK. During the process I found out that for a couple of years I had been working with fellow survivor, also a civilian worker at Collingwood, in the Officers Training Offices and, of course, I was in the Transport Section. We both lived close to one another close to the base rear gate. His name was Reg Smith and he had been a Leading Telegraphist on *Foylebank*. From the first re-union we two formed a close bond until he died in 1977.

Shortly after starting the *Foylebank* Re-Union Club Peter Davies died and Doug Bishop took over and ran it smoothly every year at Portland until diminishing numbers meant that our last re-union was held in 2001 in July. It was our 24th gathering.

As the wreck of *H.MS.Foylebank* was lying in 90 feet of water in a

H.M.S. Cambridge – opening of 'Mantle Close Range School'.
Jack Mantle's brother and sister in civilians.

Opening of the Senior Rates Mess, 'Foylebank Mess',
H.M.S. Osprey (November 1989)

strategic position inside Portland Harbour it was essential that she should be salvaged when the war was over. It proved not to be straight forward for after the battering she had received she had to be brought up in two sections. The forward section was raised in 1947 and broken up in Falmouth, Cornwall. The after section had to have bomb holes patched first and the main engines removed. When afloat ammunition barges were brought alongside and 2'500 rounds of 4 inch shells plus thousands of rounds of smaller calibre bullets were taken off. By the end of April 1952 the stern section had been towed to Grays in Essex and scrapped.

Captain W.R. Fell, R.N. wrote a book called *The Sea Surrenders*, published in 1960. I came upon this volume in which he tells of some of the wartime ships he had been in charge of salvaging including ours and I am pleased to have permission to quote from his book:

I left and went to see how things were doing in Portland Harbour. The flak-ship Foylebank, of approximately 6'000 tons deadweight had been sunk during the early years of the war at an important berth in the fleet anchorage. She was in 90 feet of water and lying on most of her damage which was largely situated in the after end. It was impossible to patch her up and lift her in one piece so it had been decided to cut her in half and then try. My predecessor had got the fore end away but the after end was not so easy. When I saw it a gale was whipping short, steep seas across Portland Harbour and it was breaking in showers of spray over the wreck whose upper deck was just above the surface. It was a dismal sight.

On board compressors were running on the highest point of the wreck, supplying four divers with air. They were down in the engine room, the fore end of which was wide open and under water. On deck a party of men were rigging derricks over Nos. 4 & 8 hatches.

The holds were one great litter of rotting stores (for her complement of 300 men) ammunition and the odd German bomb that had failed to go off. We had to clear the ballast, the mud, the stores, and bombs to make the wreck seaworthy.

The coastal salvage vessel *Kinbrace* was tackling the job and I saw that her crew were really not adequate to the task confronting them. After much trouble I persuaded the Admiralty to let us take on an emergency salvage party of 10 men. Lighters, and barges carrying empty oil drums were brought in and filled with mud which was then taken clear and dumped back into the harbour. Gerry Ransome, an expert burner, who was cutting down the superstructure, let out a yell one day and came running out.

"What's the trouble Gerry?" I inquired, and he replied, "Nothing really, I just found that instead of dead steel I was burning into live shells and you might get someone to shift them."

"Not to worry, if they didn't go off then they won't now", I told him. The divers made and fitted patches for the bomb holes and cut away the decks and gun platforms above the engine room. Once *Kilbrace* had lifted them clear the dismantling of the main engines was able to commence as they were now accessible. Even after all those years the nuts turned and bolts were withdrawn with ease. Slowly she was coming right.

At the end of February 1952 the main engines were removed down to their crankshafts and we cleared the holds and tested all compartments for water tightness. Thousands of rounds of ammunition, of 4" machine gun type were got onto barges. All was still knee deep in mud and from the ships living quarters the Hebridean divers had discovered human bones. They downed tools and all bones on board were sought and collected and taken ashore before they would continue. On 31st March Kilbrace was trying to lift the port engine crankshaft and had a weight of about 150 tons on her tackles when instead of raising the crankshaft she raised the whole stern of the wreck. We got it out a few days later.

On 10th April 1952 *Foylebank* was towed to a berth in the harbour where much of the ballast was taken out and she rode higher and higher with each load removed. Water was drained from the tunnel flats and bilges and the last parts were removed from her (parts of the engine and ballast) and she was towed to the ship breakers in the Thames, her final journey beginning on 23rd April. The last job of all we had to do was remove 20,000 tins of butter and soggy meat from the refrigerator spaces. We were not sorry to see the last of her!

(Edited highlights from *The Sea Surrenders*)

On reading the newspaper cutting and picture of *H.M.S. Foylebank* sinking in Portland Harbour after her attack by enemy aircraft, I was prompted to recall how I had 'turned over', to my relief, the duties of the motor-boat driver the night before we were bombed. It was my last trip in the boat. He was to take over my job with the first trip with the postman the next morning – the fateful 4th July 1940. I do not even recall his name, but I advised him to do what I always did – after breakfast about 7.30am, to leave the ship and go down into the motor-boat via the lower boom, and to take a book or paper to read in the covered-in engine compartment. That way he was out of the bustle of ship-board routine and ready when the crew came down for the first trip at 9am. If he did that, I have often thought... there but for the grace of God... went I!

Chapter 5

H.M.S. BULLDOG

My 14 days survivor's leave to recover from the stress of the sinking of my ship was now over, and I returned to Portsmouth and put in a request to qualify as an ASDIC Branch S/D Operator: Anti-Submarine Detector, and this was granted. The course was at Dunoon in Scotland, where trainees were introduced to the requirements and theory of submarine detection.

Having completed the introductory part of the course, which was mainly becoming familiar with the methods of detecting submarines, the theory, how and why of operational duties, and so forth. We set off across country to Campbeltown, a lovely little fishing port at the southern end of the Kintyre peninsula in Argyll. This was the wartime home of *H.M.S. Osprey* which had moved from Portland for security reasons. The base at Campbeltown was called *H.M.S.Nimrod* and it was there that we did the practical course. We learnt about the Oscillator, which was lowered into a dome fixed at the bottom of a ship, whilst it was being operated. Being a delicate instrument the oscillator would be kept raised in port or when there was a need for maintenance or change of parts.

In operation a radio beam was sent out from the ship through the water, travelling for about a mile, or less if it happened to be struck. If that happened it would return an echo to the receiver and be heard by the asdic operator as a sort of ping through his earphones, as he sat in his tiny cabinet or hut situated on the wing of the upper bridge or in a larger compartment in the bowels of the ship directly above the dome. In his bridge type Cabinet the operator was in direct contact with his Captain and other bridge personnel, but when below decks he was completely shut off and isolated by all the water-tight doors and hatches being closed and secured when operating at sea.

The unit encompassed 360 degrees and the operator would complete given 'sweeps' of so many degrees or a section, of the compass, which would be swept by automatically trained 'steps' of each transmission of the oscillator beam. Thus a given sweep area ordered by the Officer of the Watch (OOW), or other person authorised to do so, could be carried out simply by setting the sweep area and listening for any echoes or other noises. (The film *The Cruel Sea* starring Jack Hawkins, about a submarine chaser, illustrates all this very well.)

If the transmission faded as it reached its limit then the next beam was sent on its way. If at some stage an echo was heard then a solid object had most likely been 'seen' by the beam then it would need investigation to determine if it was a submarine or something else. As the operator my first task in this situation was to find the extent of the target. A submarine could be about 10 degrees in extent. Anything larger might be a school of fish or a wreck, or even a whale. These could obviously be disregarded.

Having an echo I would sweep across the target to the left in 2 degree steps until contact was lost when when I would sweep back to the right until contact was regained. At that point it would be 'right cut on', the distance between the two 'cut ons' being the distance to target, or as it was called, 'extent'. By this time the Captain would have been informed.

If we assume that the left cut was 10 degrees and the right was 20 degrees then the 10 degree 'extent' of the target could be assumed to be a submarine. If it moved as I transmitted further 'pings' then I would call out "target moving right or left" as the case may be. A submarine would be slow moving underwater and a shoal of fish faster which helped identify the 'target'.

Noises would also add clues to identity such as voices or engine sounds coming in to my earphones. Fish normally transmit whistling sounds or other noises. Surface ship sounds would be different again. The returning echo could also produce a 'doppler' effect. When the beam transmitted then the sound would disappear as the beam moved away out of range (like a car or train coming towards you and then passing and the sound fading away) but if after a short interlude a clear echo returns then the pitch will be higher than it was when first sent and lower in pitch.

So the constant flow of information coming in to the operator was given by him to the Captain and the ship would act accordingly. Its importance in submarine detection was enormous.

When carrying out convoy escort duties there would be long periods when nothing eventful took place as the asdic pinged away but one had to be alert at all times just in case. For a successful attack on a submarine - the CO would need the classification of the echo – the order to investigate would be given by him or whoever was responsible – the operator had to find the 'extent' of the target, if it was moving or still, which way it was heading, any identifying sounds – if it was not thought to be a submarine the order to disregard was given if everything was right then 'action stations' was sounded and the HSD (Higher Submarine Detector) would close up beside the operator who would need to keep the submarine in 'view' as the ship moved towards its target the information coming in to the operator would be given out so that speed and course of the ship, and depth setting of the submarine would be put on the depth charges – meanwhile the operator had to make sure he did not lose his quarry!

My next ship was *H.M.S. Bulldog* on board which I would carry out my new Submarine Detection duties. This ship had gained an impressive reputation, not least during the action off Norway when Lord Louis Mountbatten was Captain of the destroyer *H.M.S. Kelly*. The British flotilla supporting our troops ashore on the mainland had been under constant air attack by dive-bombers and Kelly had received her share of direct hits to the extent that she began to sink. *H.M.S. Bulldog* went to her aid and took off her crew, by which time the sinking destroyer had water reaching her upper decks. Mountbatten went back on board with a small crew and a tow was rigged between the two ships. Despite a couple more air attacks, and due to fine seamanship *H.M.S.Kelly* was sailed back to the UK where she was docked and repaired. Eventually she rejoined the Fleet and Lord Louis remained as her Captain until the time off Malta, when she was on escort duties and *Kelly* was once again attacked from the air but this time she was sunk. Only her Captain and a handful of men survived.

By 18th February 1941 *Bulldog* had completed another North Atlantic convoy escort job with the loss of only two merchant vessels during a period when the German 'Wolf Packs', as the groups of U-boats working together were called, were very active.

We had left the convoy and would normally be heading for bleak Scapa Flow, the Royal Navy's huge anchorage in Scotland. At that time there was little to excite weary matelots returning from the sea, other than a shore canteen and a few houses. For the past nine months we had sailed from Scapa, picked up our designated convoy, escorted it to mid-Atlantic and collected another which was coming from the United States. However, this time was different! We were entering Liverpool for a much needed boiler-clean which meant that a small number of the crew who could be spared from normal duties could be given leave as they had no shoreside duties. That meant no guns to man or duties allied to the smooth running of the ship. It so happened that on this occasion I and my shore-going pal Ordinary Seaman 'Spike ' Ellis had been lucky enough to be among those who were given leave the next day. We decided to run ashore and celebrate our long awaited break on the morrow.

That run ashore on the first night of our arrival was the most outstanding I had during my many years in the Royal Navy and it

H.M.S. Bulldog

began at 7pm when Spike and I made our way through the black-out to the centre of Liverpool where we came upon the popular pub named "The Blue Rooms". It was already quite lively when we settled ourselves at a small table in the corner of the bar room. It was pretty full, mainly with uniformed patrons and so we set out to enjoy ourselves.

An hour after we had arrived Spike said, "Those three civvies over there seem to be taking an interest in us, do you know any of them?" "Hardly likely is it", I replied, "this being my first visit here and we have just come in from the sea. Mind you one of their faces does seem familiar now you mention it!" A short while later the one I had remarked upon got up and came over. "Weren't you on the *Glasgow*?" he said to me, "and didn't you do a runner at Portsmouth before we sailed for Canada as escort to the King and Queens trips in 1938?" I replied that he was right and he went on, "I am Gibbons and l did a runner when we got to Canada, but I stayed out and am doing OK. "After a few reminiscences about *H.M.S. Glasgow* I said "You are right about me but I returned and received a Kings Pardon!" He returned to his two dubious looking companions and I recalled to Spike that I had known Gibbons as part of the crew but not well.

The evening ran its course and just prior to closing time Gibbons and his pals asked us to join them at a night club to finish our run ashore. We had sunk a few beers by then and the night was still young so we went along. Outside it was pitch black and felt un-welcoming as we followed our new 'friends' to a place named Hanover Street which we entered. A little way along we arrived at some steps leading up to a large dark painted door through which an eye peered at us via a 'peep hole'. Once the door was opened we were ushered inside along a short corridor to a large room where quite a party was going on with lots of people chattering away and drinking at side tables.

Spike and I were guided by Gibbons to the bar stools and were served a pint each and told to settle ourselves in, make ourselves comfortable, after which Gibbons rejoined his pals. There was music coming from somewhere and the atmosphere was friendly. We had sunk a lot of beer by now and were in no hurry to leave. However, Gibbons joined us again after a half hour had passed and asked if we would like to earn a fiver (5 pounds) each, a lot of money in those days and more than a weeks wage for many. Neither of us liked the sound of this but a few extra 'quid' would certainly by handy. Another of his chums came over and they said "alright then lads follow us and we will put you in the picture."

It was getting on for midnight when we left the club walking along what we found out later was Liverpool's main shopping centre, Lime Street and there seemed to be many people out and about at that hour. The two of us, both in uniform, followed these two civilians about until we came to a large recessed doorway of a shop. Gibbons said to us "Right lads, all you two have to do is stand on the pavement outside this door and don't let anyone come in." We did as he bade us and the next thing that happened was the crash of breaking glass and the two crooks disappeared inside. This was followed by a bit of thumping around and then coming and going with things being carried out and paced in the porch area. We were told to turn around holding out our arms which were stacked with bundles of something or other, so many we couldn't see over the of them.

"Right lads", said our 'pal' Gibbons, "I will lead and my mate will follow behind us. We're going back to the club. You two being in uniform and it being dark I reckon no one will take any notice of you." So off we went back down Lime Street in line ahead with Spike bringing up the rear with the 'Spiv' and me up ahead with Gibbons. Back at No 10 Hanover Street we were soon inside and unloaded and told to go to the bar and drink up, Gibbons paying for the pints. He congratulated us and paid us each a big, white fiver "as I promised", before going back to his cronies. By then our drink befuddled brains were really not working too well, making us easy meat for what came next. We couldn't make a strategic retreat anyway, not with the bouncer guarding the only exit. Then the situation changed for the worst when Gibbons suggested that we do another job for them at the same rate we were paid before. When we protested and told him we were off back to the ship he threatened us. We knew we were up to our necks in trouble already so when he said, "If you do another job for us you can go, but not before, or my mates won't like it if you refuse. You might not get back at all because anything can happen in the blackout. I will be back for you shortly when I've got my mates together." 'Spike' and I decided to go along with them and see what they were up to and then if it was another shop, when they had gone inside we could shoot off in the darkness back to the ship.

Four minutes later Gibbons was back and he told us we were going back to the same place, a well known store called Swears and Wells, the furriers. When we reached the shop and the crooks went inside all hell was let loose with whistles blowing and cars screaming to a halt and hordes of police running from all sides. We two were grabbed and hand-cuffed, as were Gibbons and his mates as they came running out to see what all the racket was about. Bundled into the rear of a Black Maria (police van) we were all driven to Lime Street police station. Both of us were in uniform, of course, and were interviewed together and informed that all would be clarified for us. One RN Officer would then be detailed to represent us on behalf of the Royal Navy in the course of all future discussions by the police with us. Then it was off to the cells to complete our first run ashore in wartime Liverpool.

Later that morning one of *H.M.S. Bulldog*'s Officers did arrive and after discussions told us that a detective would be talking to us shortly and that we were no longer attached to *Bulldog*, we would be administered by *H.M.S. Eaglet* instead. She was a Liverpool-based depot-ship at the docks.

Then began our first interview with the detective and our appointed solicitor, a woman from a local firm. The detective had the same name as myself. The solicitor was Miss Rose Heilbron. We were told that the police were not really interested in us, we were just a couple of dupes due to being befriended on our first ever time in the city, by a group of extremely unscrupulous people whom the police had been watching for some time, suspected as being active looters taking advantage of the blackout and bombing. Damaged shops were easy targets after they had been boarded up temporarily with their stock still inside.

We were held in custody, or on bail, as the courts decided, until the police completed their enquiries and arrested all of the gang. Then the trial would begin and as we were with them when they were caught we would be needed to appear along with the crooks until the presiding judge decided what he wanted to do with us. When we stood in the dock next to the looters our solicitor asked for bail in our case and it was granted so we were taken to *H.M.S. Eaglet* which was permanently secured alongside the jetty; acting as a depot ship. The Master-at-Arms received us and told us the rules of our stay during the seven days remand period, which could be extended. We would undertake normal ships company duties and at all times remain aboard under close supervision, and had to report along with men under punishment. It wasn't much of a bind really as we mixed with the crew and enjoyed ship-board life once again. What we found hard to take was not having to close up for 'action stations'.

Back at court the custody review was a shock because bail was refused by the judge who ordered that we remain in custody until our next appearance. We were hand-cuffed and led to a prison van and taken to Liverpool's notorious Walton Prison. After going through the reception room we came to another area staffed by a dozen very efficient looking prison warders. At the first table all our particulars were noted. At the next our personal items were listed after we had laid them out, they were then placed in a bag. At the following table we had to strip naked and then we were ushered into a shower room where hot water washed away the previous nights sleep. From the shower we were taken for a medical examination and then into yet another room where prison clothes were issued to us and a prison number given. Having now been separated we were now together again, on remand rather than convicted so we were dressed differently to the inmates. We had on a brown shorts and trousers with black socks and shoes.

From reception, warders took us to the prison proper where a burly warder with a huge bunch of keys led us up some iron steps to a walkway which continued around the inside of the building. Each floor was exactly the same and from them doors opened to reveal cells. We followed the 'screw', terminology for the warders, until I was told "You, go in there!", after which the heavy door was banged shut behind me. Spike was lodged in another cell.

I looked about me and a feeling of abandonment and intense solitude came over me, this last being unique to prison life. At least it was in 1941. No television, no radio, no newspapers, no games room or diversionary activities. It was supposed to be a punishment and those long hours of solitude felt like it. Every cell was the same, containing a small wooden table and chair, a wood framed bed with a thin horse-hair mattress with a blanket and hard bolster pillow. On the table was a Gideon Bible and in a corner a bucket and roll of toilet paper, our toilet arrangements. The only light came through a barred and brick lined window frame high up in the rear wall, around two feet square. We were locked in for many hours each day.

Our normal weekday began with the slamming of the doors as the warder threw them open hence prison was nicknamed the 'slammer. The sound of jangling keys accompanied this racket at 6.30am had been preceded by a warder shouting to encourage us to make a move. Now began 'slopping out' which meant that every man took his ablution bucket to the large ablution area at the far end of the block where he emptied it. We grabbed a quick wash at the basins and carried our buckets back to our cells to await the meal trolley which was brought past each cell. Breakfast was a bowl of porridge, a lump of bread, and a mug of tea which we took inside to eat, the doors being slammed behind us. We sat at our tables and ate. At 8am the doors were opened again and the dirty utensils were collected and we then pulled our tables and chairs outside onto the walk around. The sides of mail bags, thread, and sail-makers needles were brought to us and we began work until 11am.

There was constant supervision. As soon as one bag was completed another was provided and all was silence. No talking was allowed, or smoking for that matter, during working hours. I believe the remand prisoners were treated differently because on the 'convicted' wing there was a library, rest room and other facilities. We were even denied a cell mate to whom we could talk. At 11am everything was removed from us and we each placed our table and chair back in our cells, after which we were marched single file down the stairs, through reception and out into the large exercise yard where in the middle stood an armed warder. We strolled around in a circle until 15 minutes had passed when we were taken back inside. This was the same morning and afternoon, day in day out.

Back in our cells the doors were slammed shut until 12.30 when a dinner was passed into our cells. This usually consisted of thin soup with a few vegetables and a lump of meat. A mug of water washed it down. On occasion we had a dessert of sponge pudding and custard.

The forenoon routine was repeated after 'lunch' until our day ended at 3.30pm with an exercise period and tea in the cell, this was a mug of tea instead of water and sandwiches, perhaps. At 4pm we were locked up again until next morning and the routine began again. It was all so frustrating with no way to occupy ones mind. In the dark hours I could see searchlights and flashes of bombs exploding or ack ack guns firing defined by the small, high, window as Liverpool was pasted by enemy bombers. The drone of the aircraft made it all seem lonelier somehow. Sometimes the bombing was uncomfortably close. Nearby air raid sirens would moan and wail. If we happened to be out of our cells when the sirens went we would be hurried back to them and locked in. We were never put in air raid shelters. The two short spells I had at Walton prison included at least one direct hit which produced casualties. We were lucky in that the Remand Wing was spared that.

My first spell in Walton prison was for just a week then followed another court appearance and we were informed by our solicitor that the next court appearance was a month hence and that a number of arrests had been made so that the trial could begin then. After a further week at Walton we were transferred to Strangeways Prison at Manchester. Routines were similar. Once more we had single cells. The air raids were just as bad as at Liverpool.

We were at Manchester a week prior to the Manchester Assizes commencing but the prison received a direct hit in that time and a convicted murderer was hanged. Life was not quite so boring!

When the big day arrived 'Spike' and I were brought to reception and dressed in our uniforms and had our possessions given back and we were loaded into a 'Black Maria' for the journey to court and placed in a holding cell as we waited for the case to begin.

It was a large court we brought into from the cells area below, with witnesses and the public seated in front and to the rear the bewigged judge and court officials. Promptly at 10 am Mr Justice Hallett entered; there were seven accused civilians and the two of us in uniform all standing together. Procedures were completed and the trial began with the judge stating "Before we go any further I want those two sailors removed from among those criminals as they are not criminals but, in my book, heroes." "Blimey!" I thought! Rose Heilbron (much later to become Judge Heilbron) accompanied us to our seats alongside the witnesses, where we remained for the rest of the trial. By noon those in the dock had been charged with looting and other offences, were found guilty, and given prison sentences ranging from 3 to 7 years. Spike and I were told we were free to go and were escorted back to *H.M.S.Eaglet* where we were given a hot meal, a rail warrant to Portsmouth and told to make our way there and report to the Regulating Office at R.N.B.

Before we left *Eaglet* we were able to see and say thank you, and goodbye, to Rose Heilbron who was a very special lady who gave me the impression that she would do well by her chosen profession, as she did. I read in my local appear that in 1956 she had become Britain's first female judge.

After a long weekend leave I returned to Portsmouth to find a draft chit waiting for me, to join *H.M.S.Windsor* on 15th April 1941.

Due to unforeseen circumstances, previously recounted, I could not sail with *H.M.S.Bulldog* when, after her boiler-clean, she returned to Scapa Flow to resume her Atlantic convoy escort-duties. My former shipmates experienced an historic trip for them, when they were escorting a convoy south of Greenland in the Atlantic a short while later. On May 9th 1941 two merchant ships in their convoy were torpedoed and sunk and when the periscope of a submarine was sighted it was attacked by *H.M.S. Aubretia*, a corvette, who dropped ten depth-charges on it. A little later *H.M.S. Bulldog*, under the command of Captain J. Baker-Cresswell who was the Senior Officer of the convoy-escorts, was about to make his depth-charge attack when they were all surprised to see the U110 surface. German sailors, appeared to be manning their gun so *Bulldog* opened fire on them and then they abandoned their submarine and jumped into the sea, including their Captain who was not rescued or seen again, it was assumed that he had drowned. The usual practice in these circumstances was to ram the submarine and sink it. *Bulldog*'s Captain was about to do just that when, seeing the submarine still there and apparently with no one on board, he decided to board it with, an armed boarding party and take it as a prize. A boarding party of around eight men, under the orders of Sub Lieutenant Balme approached the submarine in *Bulldog*'s sea boat and Sub. Lieutenant Balme boarded the U110 to determine the situation.

Alone and very apprehensive, he went down an upper-deck hatch into the depths of the submarine – not an enviable task because he did not know if there was anyone below who may be armed, or even if any 'self-destruct' explosives had been set-up down there.

Having satisfied himself that there was nobody below, he told the boarding party to join him and to collect all the charts, decoding and signal manuals – in fact everything that might be of interest to our boffins. Whilst that was being done one of the boarding party Leading Telegraphist Allan Long asked Sub Lieutenant Balme to come to the Wireless Office and view a rather mysterious - looking piece of typewriter-type equipment. It looked very much like a type-writer but when the keys were pressed different illuminated letters showed up Sub. Lieutenant Balme told Leading Telegraphist Long to unscrew the four 'holding-down' screws and take it, together with all the instruction and other written, relevant books up on the deck and put them into *Bulldog*'s sea boat. When the boarding-party got back on the U110's upper-deck they found they were on their own on an abandoned German U-boat somewhere in the Atlantic Ocean. Apparently *H.M.S Bulldog* had gone off to

H.M.S. Bulldog's seaboat, with boarding party approaching U110
(reproduced by permission Imperial War Museum)

investigate another U-boat in the vicinity of the convoy, having dealt with that emergency, *Bulldog* later returned for the boarding party, much to their relief, and hoisted the sea boat. As the U110 was still afloat, Captain Baker-Cresswell decided to take her in tow and see if he could get it back to Scapa Flow. It was not to be however, for eventually the U-boat began to sink by the bows – so the tow was slipped and U110 sank to the bottom of the Atlantic – but minus all the secret papers and other equipment that was now safely stowed in *Bulldog*'s Radio office.

Experts from Bletchley Park were waiting at Scapa Flow when *H.M.S. Bulldog* entered harbour and were extremely pleased with what they collected and took back with them. Thanks to the capture of that Enigma machine the British Navy were able to know where most groups of U-boats were and steered convoys away from them. Sinkings dropped dramatically, among our convoys. In 1970 when the government released official wartime records the true story of what happened when the U110 was sunk, came to light.

Shortly after the U110 event, those concerned were told that they were to be awarded medals for their part in the capture and sinking of U110. Captain J. Baker-Cresswell received the D.S.O., Sub. Lieutenant David Balme, received the D.S.C. and Leading Telegraphist Allan Long received the D.S.M.

Chapter 6

H.M.S. WINDSOR

I joined *H.M.S. Windsor* in Portsmouth Dockyard on 15th April 1941. She was numbered D42 and was one of the V&W Class.Destroyers from World War I of which there were several still in service at that time, two of which were *H.M.S. Walpole* and *H.M.S.Whitshead.*They were very easily identified by their two funnels the forrard of which was like a long 'Woodbine' cigarette the after one being shorter and fatter. On board they carried 2 × 4.5 inch guns forrard and 1 × 4.5 aft.

They had come to almost the end of their useful lives but were badly needed, as we had lost so many ships to German aggression and were fighting for our lives against the stranglehold of starvation. Convoy escorts were worth their weight in gold! Full use was made of them in both convoy and patrol duties.

Based at Portsmouth our duties at first were mainly English Channel patrols where there was plenty of activity throughout the war. Germany occupied the Normandy coast of France and had taken over the submarine pens and important coastal ports which they used to the full. Shipping going through the English Channel, heading for German ports was often due our attention. Against this the enemy had many fast surface attack craft called 'E Boats' and we had many encounters with these formidable vessels.

Often, on patrol, convoy escort, or attack mission the Captain would often tannoy the crew about whatever we were about so that we were prepared at all times for action. The Channel actions and incidents were fairly frequent and always interesting. One such occasion comes to mind. We had left Portsmouth Harbour and were in our patrol area when, at 2.45 am the Captain came on the inter-com to tell us we had been made aware of a small German convoy making its way towards and past Dover and "we are now increasing speed so as to be in contact range." 'Action stations' was piped and we closed up.

My 'action station' was in the Wardroom. The magazine for the after-gun was below their deck, access to it being via a hatch beside which I stood, on a table, my head and upper torso through the gun deck hatch above I would have to pass shells through. This upper hatch was directly under the breech of the 'after gun'. Down in the darkness the magazine crew had to pass the shells up to a chap in the Wardroom from whom I would grab them and hand them up to the gun crew who then shoved it into the breech and it was sent on its way to the enemy. The re-coil of the gun firing brought the breech back over my head. My 'action station' then, was half below decks and half above decks. A strange place indeed. I was in this position when closed up and able to give a running commentary of all that I saw to the lads below who saw nothing.

At about 3.15am we were informed over the intercom that we were now in range of the enemy and the gun crews should load and stand by to engage the enemy. Once the action started it was all go as the 'after gun' fired I handed the ammunition up to willing hands, wait-ed for the gun to fire and recoil just above my head and the whole thing was done again and again and so on. I was just shouting to the lads below when the action hotted up as I spotted two E Boats com-ing for us with guns blazing. I told the lads down there in the red glow of the night lighting. "I can see the flashes of their guns, trac-er is coming at us. We have been hit in our funnels".

There was a slight lull in the fighting and the Wardroom lads, who were looking up at me, suddenly seemed very concerned about my well-being. "Are you all right Ron? Have you been wounded?" I told them, "Not that I know of, why?"

"Because there is blood on your face." I brushed my hand across my face and sure there was something sticky and warm on the back of my hand. Then suddenly we were in action again and I yelled "pass up the ammo – there's a fleet of ships nearby – they seem to be having some hits from our guns – there's an E Boat coming at us again – its stopped in its tracks – it has had a direct hit!"

From the lads below came "Ron, are you sure you're alright – do you want a relief from up there?" I could feel that stickiness on my lower face and neck now. I said to them "I seem to be OK at the moment – it looks we will break off the action soon so I will stand fast."

Shortly after this we were stood down from 'action stations'. They piped 'Hands to cruising stations' I came down from the table, into the Wardroom where the lads anxiously waited to rush me to the sick bay. I took my steel helmet off and we started to investigate. One of the lads rubbed his hands on my face then, after careful study, said "Its bloody oil by the smell of it!" On further investigation we spotted a tin lying on its side beside the gun's breech. It was an empty oil tin that had been full when left beside the breech from the last "quarters clean guns". With the recoil from the start of the action the can had fallen and its contents dripped on to me, and in the red glow of the lamps in the wardroom it had looked like blood. So much for a D.S.M. (Distinguished Service Medal). Try again Ron!

From the Portsmouth area we were moved to Harwich for escort duties through 'E boat alley' in the North Sea. Our base was Harwich at the Southern end of England where we would see the convoys through to Immingham at the entrance to the Humber. It was particularly narrow at that part of the North Sea, and just a step away from the E boat bases. Invariably, soon after assembly the convoys would be attacked by E boats, which would dart in and out at high speed firing torpedoes and guns, which would usually sink a ship or two. However, our bigger guns were not idle and we gave a

H.M.S. Windsor

good account of ourselves, so the E boats would not press home attacks as we shot one or two of them.

We kept quite busy up to Immingham with a north bound convoy and back to Harwich with a south bound one. A convoy with a different aspect happened when we left Harwich to escort a northbound convoy on what began as a murky morning. We had not been long underway, with four other escorts around the larger than usual number of ships when a few E boats made a short and desultory attack during the afternoon which thankfully was uneventful. Then the fog closed down, visibility dropped to zero and with all those ships around it was now a different mission for us all, one of survival. Being in a pea-souper is no joke at the best of times but at sea, in such circumstances it was horrendous.

Sometimes the warning sound of a ship's hooter could be heard but that did not tell you the direction as sound was absorbed by the droplets which made up the fog. After a couple of sandwiches and a mug of tea for my midday meal I looked around at a blank wall of greyness and decided it might be wise to get an hours 'kip' while I could.

I got myself a long mess stool, set it down on the upper deck under cover from the overhead of the canteen flat. I settled myself along its 14" width, got my head down and the next thing I knew was a terrific jolt and I found myself lying on the deck. There was the sound of irregular scraping, of iron on iron. Our engines were stopped and there were sounds of voices shouting orders or asking "What's up?" I got to my feet and began to walk along the starboard side deck towards the stern.

The fog was still thick and as I passed mid-ships the creaking got worse and suddenly I found myself walking into a huge wall of steel. Peering upwards I could see a row of faces looking downwards and it dawned on me that a huge American Liberty Ship was well and truly through our starboard side by about ten feet. It took another half hour before she then slid astern and shook herself free from us. I heard muffled exchanges between our bridge and theirs. One remark was "Sorry about that – hope you make it OK." Then all was silence again. Those of us who were available made ourselves useful clearing up the debris and positioning a collision mat over the gash in the ship's side, which was mostly above the water line.

The largest casualty was the 'rum-store', the door having been ripped off and a few broken jars littered the deck. The Officer of the Watch promptly detailed an acting P.O. and an AB to stay on duty in front of the rum store until we reached harbour. Some five hours later we arrived back at Harwich where they welded a steel plate over the gash as a temporary measure. Two days later we made our way up north to Immingham once more and were placed in dry-dock where a permanent repair was made.

On 22nd May 1941 we were back as 'fully operational' with orders to join *H.M.S. Hood* up north as an extra escort which made a change for us from interminable escort in 'E boat alley.' It was well into the night when we were alerted to the fact that there was something afoot, everything was silent. Then we realised that we were wallowing helplessly, out of control in the choppy seas somewhere south of Iceland. Our orders were to make good our engine repairs, if able, and endeavour to get to Reykjavik, Iceland.

By noon on 22nd May 1941 we were arriving in Icelandic waters and soon were going alongside to get our engines properly fixed up. They were beginning to show their age but still doing a grand job of work. It was as we worked on the engines that we heard the shocking news. *H.M.S.Hood*, the 'Mighty Hood', had blown up with all but three of her ships company of 1421 men killed. Only three survivors – didn't bear thinking about! It was a blow to the morale of the Navy and the British people! We completed our repairs and once again fully operational we made our way back to Harwich and resumed our work in 'E boat alley'.

On the last of our occasional weekend breaks in Portsmouth Dockyard I got a draft chit for R.N.B. Portsmouth, so I packed my bags and left *H.M.S.Windsor* on 6th June 1941.

Chapter 7

OPERATION TORCH

During my stay at RNB Portsmouth I decided that it might be a good opportunity to put in a request to qualify for the course of H.S.D. (Higher Submarine Detector) which, if granted would also give me an assured spell in the UK, at *H.M.S. Osprey* in Dunoon, and at *H.M.S. Campbeltown*, both in Scotland. *Osprey* had moved to Scotland from Dorset to carry out her training task in greater safety from bombing attacks.

A few days later it was a case of forget HSD when I found a draft chit waiting for me when I returned to the Mess. It told me simply to report to the drafting office to arrange my going to *H.M.S. Acute*. On 8th July 1942 a contingent of 60 Senior and Junior Rates with two Officers left Portsmouth by train for Belfast where our new berth was waiting. She had been built by Messrs. Harland & Wolff in their Belfast shipyard and we were to be her first crew after acceptance trials. Almost 100 of this type of Fleet Minesweeper were built during the war years, to supplement the converted trawlers which were the mainstay of the minesweeping fleet. They were regarded as being the fastest and most efficient of their type. Many were sold abroad after the war to the navies of Belgium, South Africa, Burma, Ceylon, Greece, Nigeria, Persia, and Thailand.

After we had gone on board we settled down to get acquainted with each other and the ship. My particular interest being the anti-submarine equipment, termed ASDIC, whose dome was situated on the ship's bottom some 40 feet back from her bow. The ASDIC cabinet nested in the starboard corner of the bridge. We commissioned

H.M.S. Acute on 9th July and after approval of her trials we left Belfast on the 31st for Tobermory Bay in Scotland where working up trials would commence and last for two weeks. The crew learned to work together and become used to their new watches and the 101 other things they needed to know and to do to fight the ship efficiently.

At the start we met up with a little man of great reputation. On duty he was a 'Holy Terror' and one always wondered what unpleasantness he had up his sleeve next. Off duty he was quite a pleasant Naval Officer known as Commodore Norman Stephenson RN, later to become a Vice Admiral with KBE, CB, and CMB after his name. An Officer not part of a ship's company was always appointed as a referee during a work up to put the ship and crew impartially through their paces. This officer was destined to take over as Senior Naval Officer Working Up Trials, Tobermory, a Scottish town on the shore of a near land locked bay of the same name. It was an ideal place in wartime for such trials to be conducted away from enemy eyes.

The Commodore's flagship, *H.M.S. Western Isles*, was an old ship adapted for its role. Every ship arriving for trials very soon got to know this officer very well indeed. He gained a reputation as well as a number of nicknames which held a certain irreverence but which were destined to catch on. He was elderly and short in stature with a really loud voice, and side burns down his chin which earned him the nickname 'Monkey face'. He was already known as the 'Tobermory Terror' and 'Puggy'.

After a full days work which began the hour you arrived you would anchor in the Bay and after 'pipe down' when all was still at 3am, 'Action Stations' would be sounded when much cursing and mumbling from the crew accompanied their stumbling towards their posts, timed by 'The Terror'. Suddenly the Commodore would show himself, dressed in his 'posh' rig, and would throw down his heavily gold braided cap onto the deck in front of some luckless sailor and shout "INCENDIARY BOMB". The startled matelot would be glowered at and the question thrown at him "WELL, WHAT ARE YOU GOING TO DO ABOUT IT?" The correct action was to kick it over the side. The 'Terror' would then shout "MAN OVERBOARD, AWAY STARBOARD SEABOAT, COL-LECT MAN OVERBOARD (the cap) AND RETURN TO ME!" A couple of hours pandemonium would ensue until he would suddenly decide "EXERCISE COMPLETE!" We would fall out and secure.

By the time our two weeks was up we were far wiser and a more disciplined crew, fully conversant with our equipment, what it was all for and where it was stowed, who did what and when, and why. By now we had got to know one another very well, had sorted out shore going 'oppos' or 'chums', friendships which survived the passage of time. I had one such 'oppo' called John Pettigrew and I last saw him in 1943 when I did a 'pierhead jump' in Phillipville, North Africa.

In the *Navy News* of December 1998 I placed an 'Over To You' request for two shipmates I knew on *H.M.S. Glasgow* in 1937. They were asked to contact me but I never heard from either of them, except that John Pettigrew telephoned me. It appeared that for all those intervening years we had lived only 20 miles apart. We met up and enjoyed recalling events we had both been a party to 55 years before. As this is written (2003) we are still in contact and meet regularly.

After Tobermory came Rosyth Command at Port Edgar where our final work-up consisted mainly of mine-sweeping, streaming and recovering sweeps, fitting paravanes and cutters and kites, etc. In general we learned to sweep mines effectively! We sailed into Harwich on 28th September 1942 and sailed out again on the 12th October, but this time as Flotilla Leader of 12th M/S Squadron. With us we had *H.M.S. Alegerine, Alarm* and *Albacore* on passage to the Clyde via a very rough passage through the Pentland Firth,

*Left to right: Able Seaman Archibald, Able Seaman Pettigrew,
Able Seaman Walsh and Leading Seaman Harby*

arriving at Rothesay on the 22nd. Two days later we were at sea
again among scores of ships both Naval and Merchant Marine, as
part of the escort. Other vessels would join the convoy and escort
later, the Captain informed us over the tannoy. We were part of a
huge invasion force which included many American ships of all
types. Soon the Rock of Gibraltar was in sight ahead of us and we
knew that this enormous, spectacular, conglomeration of ships with
its aircraft carriers, and air escort above us, was ready for something
serious.

As we prepared to enter the Straits of Gibraltar and head into the
Mediterranean our Captain informed us that we would soon clear
lower decks when he would inform us fully of the invasion and our

part in it. It was evening on the 7th November 1942 and "we are about to invade North Africa", he said, "with landings taking place at both Oran and Algiers. Our objective is to take Algiers but this will not be straightforward for two main reasons. Firstly, it is commanded by a Vichy French garrison and it is not known how the French General will react. He might resist or he may welcome us. Whatever happens it is our task to sweep a channel for the invasion fleet, into Algiers Harbour." This meant, of course, that we would be close to the shore and under the guns of the French who might or might not fire at us from the several known, large gun emplacements ashore. At that range we would be sitting targets.

Added to that little problem there was the fact that we would also be in line-ahead formation, with our sweeps out and we could not be diverted from the task in hand and we would be going along that mile in the dark. "Good luck chaps" the C.O. said as he dismissed us.

It was a long day as we prepared ourselves and the equipment for the exercise that night. Then came the hour and it was "OUT SWEEPS" and we were off into the blackness. Thankfully we were not opposed. A destroyer had previously 'crashed' the boom which was across the harbour entrance and as soon as we reached it, it was "IN SWEEPS" and we sailed to our allotted berths in Algiers Harbour and secured alongside. By then activity was increasing and I was one of a party of six who were ordered into "boots and gaiters", with belt and holster, and told to draw revolvers and ammunition. We were a landing party under a Sub Lieutenant who ordered us to "Fall in on the jetty."

Our particular task was certainly an eye opener for me, for it was clear that the dockside brothels of any Germans who may be lingering. A couple of lorries were commandeered and were drawn up close by so that any prisoners could be escorted to them. Events certainly changed quickly. A few hours ago we were steaming along the coast in darkness wondering if we would be blasted out of the water as we swept a channel for the invasion force and now we were wandering around dockside brothels. 'Join the Navy to see the world and enjoy adventure', so the recruiting posters said.

We had a mixed reception at each of the brothels, either they were pleased to see us or they weren't. It all depended upon their loyalties to Vichy or to a Free France. As we approached each door our officer would hammer on it and wait for the cover over the little spy hole to be swung back and an eye to peer at us. If the door was opened straight away the girls would run out and fling their arms around everyone, shouting, "You English!" or something similar, then we went in, searched the rooms thoroughly and any of the enemy we found were brought out at gunpoint and marched away for interrogation. The occasions when our reception was frosty was an excuse for a more thorough search. Our mission was soon over and we were more than glad to get back to the ship early in the morning for a few hours of much needed rest.

Next day, 8th November, we had an early start. Everything had gone surprisingly well for us despite the several gun shots we had heard when we first arrived at the jetty, so Algiers was now well and truly under Allied command. It was a different story at 9am when "ACTION STATIONS' was sounded as a large formation of enemy bombers put in an appearance and proceeded to dive-bomb the ships of the convoy which were sheltering within the huge confines of Algiers Bay which adjoined the harbour. All ships which were able and that included ourselves on board *H.M.S. Acute*, steamed around firing at the intruders with every weapon we could muster. It was a hectic time while it lasted. I never did hear what damage the Germans inflicted on the ships, if any, or what we did to them in return but we were certainly OK and so returned to the harbour and secured alongside once again. From that point on it was a case of continuing to fulfil our mission which was to clear all minefields along the North African Coast.

There were three coastal towns along our route, Bougie, Phillipville, and Bone. There was also Bizerta about 200 miles from Algiers with the other three in between. Mostly we swept during the day and anchored overnight, although we occasionally called in at one or other of the towns for fuel or some other reason. The enemy had a habit of turning up to bomb any and all targets, especially ships in harbour. The following months were spent doing our main job of minesweeping, with the added order to watch out for torpedoes from lurking Italian submarines, as well as air attacks.

In the early days there *H.M.S. Algerine*, the first 'Senior Officer' of the Flotilla, was torpedoed and sunk with heavy loss of life. Later on *H.M.S. Alarm* was bombed while in Bone Harbour. We experienced the usual problems which one came across in mine-sweeping operations due to a blunt cutter on the sweep wire so that the mines anchor wire was not cut through and the sweeper would be left towing the mine and sinker rather than leaving the latter behind on the sea bed. What we did then was detach from the sweep leg and steam away from the rest of the flotilla behind us, carrying out a series of 'full stop' and 'fast go' manoeuvres which we hoped would jerk the cutter through the cable so that the mine would be released to the surface where it would be exploded by gunfire, allowing us to rejoin our comrades.

On one occasion the above efforts proved fruitless but our standby technique didn't. We heaved in on the winch until we were able to attach a line to the mine mooring wire and hoist it to the top of the davit directly over the stern. Two of us then took turns to hacksaw through the mine anchor cable, one eye on the mine, until the Minesweeping Officer was confident that it would break through with a few jerks. Having removed the hoisting line and paid out the sweep wire a few fast jerks brought the mine to the surface and rifle fire was used to explode it!

When we were sweeping off Bone another interesting job came up. As coxswain of the seaboat I was piped to report to the Captain on the bridge. "I've a job for you", he told me, "in the seaboat." He pointed towards the shore some distance away and said "Do you see that sweeper on the beach, about a quarter of a mile away? Well, when we are on the next leg we will slip you from the falls at the nearest distance between us and the beached sweeper. When you get there you should be able to get alongside or across her stern where someone on board will pass down her 'Red-Secret' charts and other items. Anything they give you bring back to us. Judge your return so that you will be able to come alongside us, hook on the falls, and we will hoist you back on board." I hadn't said anything so he looked at me quizzically and knew what was on my mind. "Don't worry about the minefield because you only draw two feet of water in the seaboat and the mines are six feet down. Your bowman will be spotting from up forrard and can see through this clear water and keep an eye out for anything which might cause a problem." Some speech but perfectly straightforward when you come to think about it of course.

The whole operation was undertaken and concluded in a satisfactory manner. I learned later how the minesweeper had come to be on the beach. Apparently *H.M.S. Alarm*, for it was she, that had been attacked by dive bombers in Bone harbour and when ordered out to sea, despite being hit she made it only to be hit again and badly damaged. Being irreparable she had been beached.

During this period when we were in Algiers harbour for a few hours one day 'Sea duty men' was piped at 9am. Two hours later we were sailing out of harbour at which point four of us were told to report to the Gunnery Office where we were issued with belts, holsters, gaiters, and signed for revolvers and ammunition. We were to be a guard party and our instructions were that an Italian submarine had been sunk by a Coastal Command aircraft and there were a large number of sailors in the water swimming in oil, probably with wounded and shocked men among them. Our ships task was to pick them out of the water and give any medical aid necessary as we returned to Algiers where the prisoners would be handed over to the authorities. The spot where the aircraft had sunk the submarine was

H.M.S. Acute during 'Operation Torch' in the North African invasion

only 20 miles away so we were soon at the spot. We four were to work with our Sick Berth Attendant (SBA) and also make sure that the prisoners made no trouble.

We lowered the seaboat as soon as we reached the spot and our lads were soon hauling oil covered men on board. Back at the ship the large minesweeping mess had been cleared and it was there that the Italian sailors were deposited. Our SBA, Norman Chapman was impressive as he dealt with these men. He was only a junior in his branch and we had no doctor on board so the responsibility was his alone. I did not envy him his task as he sorted filthy soaking men into priorities for treatment especially with a language difficulty to cope with as well. When my party returned from having a short break we saw that the prisoners were laid out on tables, stripped now so that their oil soaked bodies could be worked on. Men were moaning, several used rosaries as though their lives depended upon moving the beads from finger to finger and reciting whatever it is that Catholics recite at such times. One chap had his left leg supported above his body, the bottom part of his left foot hanging from his toes. Others appeared to have broken limbs which 'Doc' had splinted. What an appaling sight. No glamour of warfare here. We felt so sorry for them. When a couple of our lads brought in a few loaves of bread these men eagerly grabbed them and pulled them apart they were so ravenous, stuffing the lumps into their mouths.

While we stood there 'Doc' told us he needed our help. "Most of these men have oil down their guts and its making them want to spew it up so will you take a couple at a time up to the forrard heads and see if they can get the oil up?"

No problem", I said, "where do we start?" He pointed to a group.

"With that lot, they aren't injured but are retching a lot." When we approached this group and made known what we wanted to do they ignored us so we had to practically carry them and shove the first four along the narrow corridor until it dawned on us that dressed as we were in boots and gaiters, with pistols holstered on our belts they probably thought that we were going to bump them off. From their point of view as the enemy it was probably a reasonable assumption. However, having dealt with and then returned the first few, now feeling a little better, their shipmates realised that we were helping them and were not meaning any harm. Anyway, the Doc had surely proved that. We had no further bother from them after that. By the time we had finished helping them all the ship was nearing Algiers. Once alongside the prisoners were transferred to the officials waiting on the dockside. Most of the most ill or worst wounded were put into several ambulances. Another job well done!

Back we went into normal patrol routine, either sweeping mines or undertaking escort duties with convoys visiting North African ports, some of which we were now familiar with, such as Algiers, Bougie, Bone and Phillipville. With the ship alongside at Bougie one day, to pick up stores, I was working on the starboard seaboat. It was about 11.30am, the weather was hot and sunny, the sky azure blue. John Pettigrew my shore-going 'oppo' stopped for a 'natter'. After a few minutes he said, "Look at that Petty Officer among the Arabs on the jetty, he seems a bit odd don't you think?"

There was a bloke wearing PO's rig alright, and he had a thick beard, and was looking up at us. He was somehow familiar, as he should have been, being my brother John. I hadn't any idea he was in the navy, as far as I knew he was a skilled engineer on war work in a reserved occupation and employed in Lymington in the 'Wellworthy' Company. Our First Lieutenant appeared on the scene and invited my brother on board. We all got acquainted and it appeared that John's ship was anchored in the nearby bay. He asked Lt. Geen our No 1, if he could take me and my 'oppo' ashore for a short while. There was no leave due because we were to end our stay in harbour soon, but Lt. Geen said that if my brother promised to have us back on board by 4pm we could go. We had a most interesting three and a half hours ahead of us. Firstly we peered from the cliff top into the bay but could see no Royal Navy ships only a two masted sailing vessel. "That's the one I am in" said my brother, "the two master over there."

A dinghy picked us up and we soon approached the ship and scrambled aboard. What a surprise! An introduction to the civilian gentleman who turned out to be the Captain, a RN Lt.Commandcr. Below decks was even more surprising because several Royal Marines were there. They were almost ready to complete a special job they had been working on for some time, and then the ship would be heading back to the UK. Disguised as a fishing vessel the two-master had entered various bays and beaches, collecting samples and taking measurements of sea beds, beach, and cliff sizes and make up. We made no further enquires because they were on secret work.

Back on shore John told us he was taking us to meet some local friends of his and he hailed a taxi and off we went inland for a couple of miles until we came to an imposing building where we were ushered inside for a meal with an Arab Sheik and his family, the women being veiled and courteous. We ate the meal whilst all seated on the floor and were waited on by the women as is the custom. John told us that we must not refuse any of the food though there may be sheep's eyes amongst the dishes offered. That would be an insult. We had no intention of offending anyone. My brother conversed in French with our hosts. It was so pleasant away from the war for a little while but now it was time for a taxi ride back to our ship. We all said our farewells and John left for his ship and we for ours. John's ship was sailing for home on the morrow and this would be the last time I ever saw him. His last words were "See you there." But he was drowned in a boating accident in Falmouth just before he was to take home leave after being away for 16 months!

For those of us on *H.M.S. Acute* it was back to convoy duties and minesweeping again until another incident changed our routine a few weeks later.

It was early February 1943 and we were escorting a convoy. After an eventful day I was off watch from my ASDIC duties, settled quite comfortably along a wooden stool (I should have known better after the last time I did that) in the overhang of the minesweeping mess-deck. I was half asleep but with that 'ready for anything' tension we had in wartime which affects the sailor. We were suddenly flung to the deck by a huge thud. The ship appeared to be jumping up and down as I lay there partly stunned, until a quiet seemed to descend and there came a definite feeling of a change in the ship's progress. There was a noticeable pitching, irregular but there, in its up and down motion.

It turned out that a submarine had fired one or more torpedoes at us and the bridge look-out, or duty asdic operator had reported a "torpedo bearing........ Sir!" As soon as the Captain, on the bridge, received that information and satisfied himself that it was true he then ordered an immediate change of course so that the bows of the ship were facing the incoming direction of the 'tin-fish', to reduce the 'extent of target' (us) to either side of the bows, or from the length of the vessel which was 225 feet long and 35 feet in width. That evening we had not quite swung to the 'bows on' position before the torpedo arrived, travelled the whole length of the port side until presented with, and bending, the port 'A' bracket and being then swept aside and downwards by the port side propeller had then disappeared into the distance still seeking a target and leaving us with a damaged propeller and 'A' bracket which needed urgent dockyard attention. We were immediately detached from the convoy and dispatched to Gibraltar.

After about a month of repairs at 'Gib' it was back to Algiers for us and normal duties with the 12th Minesweeping Flotilla. Life carried on pretty much as usual although there was an added and most welcome break in Phillipville when I and John Pettigrew, along with a couple of other 'oppos' had a four hour run ashore.

Towards the end of June 1943 we had just completed an escort job when, at around noon, we had to go to Bone Harbour to collect stores and mail. The day was hot and just as we were securing alongside I noticed a seeming mirage. On the jetty, apparently awaiting our arrival was a fully booted and spurred sailor complete with kit-bag and hammock. A few of us remarked that it was odd for a rating to be joining a new (to him) ship, especially in a place like Bone which was at the time way up in the 'front line' with its attendant alerts and air attacks. However, I was the one who got the shock an hour later whilst working on the motor boat when the 'Jimmy' came to me and said, "Walsh, I have a surprise for you. Your relief has just come on board and you are to return to the UK We are leaving harbour in an hour so you need to get your kit packed and be on the jetty with your bag and hammock in half that time. I can't tell you what exactly the situation is ashore but I am told that there is a nearby street with several bungalows in it. In the garden of one of them is a pole with a white ensign aloft signifying that it is our temporary naval barracks. When you get there report to the Sub-Lieutenant in charge who will make arrangements to transport you back to Algiers, then on to a troopship and home.

I eventually found the bungalow as described and where I was told that there were a few others like me waiting for transport back to Algiers but it might take a while, there being only a single line coastal railway where the priority is American Army transport and stores for the British 8th Army. It might take us a few days to do the 200 mile route when we were eventually able to leave Bone. This is due to being shunted into sidings along the route while waiting for supply trains to pass. In the meantime we were to assemble each day at the flag pole each sunrise and sunset. Otherwise we just had to be available for any eventuality and were left more or less to our own devices.

On the third day the Sub said to me he had a job for me. "There will be some POWs arriving for work details and we are putting them to clearing the bomb damage at the local school which the last German air raid caused." That was fair enough but I had no idea of their 'lingo'. "How do I give them orders if I can't speak their language, Sir? And will there be the same number at the end of the day?" The Sub said, "All taken care of Walsh, so I've been told." When the prisoners arrived they were all subdued having been marched from wherever they had come from, by one of their own NCOs, a Corporal I think he was. He knew enough English for us to get by. I was required to be with them during their working day but I left all the orders, etc. to the 'bod' in charge. He marched them off to the school and they got stuck in. The NCO said, "Come", and he showed me the ground floor room set up with chairs and a table etc where he suggested that I could rest while they did the work and where he could find me if he needed to, which suited me. The main idea was to do something to prevent boredom setting in. Those Italians were no friend of the Germans who were now ex Allies, and I had no problems with them during those three days.

On the third day I was told by the Sub that five of us were to begin our journey the following day. Our transport was cattle trucks whose doors we pushed back on either side to allow a breeze in as the train and its six trucks 'tootled' along. Two days later we had travelled 190 miles and reached Algiers after stops which were of several hours duration at a time. Travelling like that was certainly very interesting and it was not long before we found out why warnings had been given that we might be longer on the journey than we thought. Every couple of hours we were pulled into sidings, waited a while, then heard the rattle and whistle of an approaching train then a very long line of high-sided trucks piled high with cargo of one sort or another would rattle and shudder to a stop alongside us for an hour or so.

The boxes which formed the cargo of each flat-bed were filled with food and fruit. There were also part open crates of large tins of fruit such as pears, oranges, and peaches which compared to our meagre rations, now long since eaten, were manna from heaven. We persuaded several of those to join us on our journey. This was not an easy task as each truck had, at each end, an American soldier dedicated to stopping thieving by the local population. One sat watching us as we worked out a plan to liberate some tins. "Hi-ya Yank, hows tricks?" He was not a friendly man. He just said "Lay off the stores, Limey, or it will give me great pleasure to use this baby," holding up his rifle in both hands. We looked at each other: "Our Allies!" we thought. Of course there was a great amount of pilfering and black market going on often with US soldiers doing the stealing and selling so these GIs were under threat of their own officers that they faced serious disciplinary problems if they failed in their duty.

It looked to be a non-starter, or at least a little more difficult than we assumed. So be it. We would do it the hard way. Two of our number slipped out of the opposite door away from the prying eyes of the Yank and made their way along the track until level with our truck. They crawled beneath the American truck as the three of us left on board attempted to keep the soldier busy. He knew what was on our minds, but not how we intended to achieve it, so he watched us closely making constant reference to death, ours. Such a nice chap. Anyway, he convinced us of his intentions I can tell you! Meanwhile our 'oppos' had got three tins already from the crate immediately above them and were in the process of crawling back the few feet to our truck along the blind side away from the guard. Once back inside, the tins were stowed under our hammocks in a corner. The 8th Army wouldn't even know they had gone and we were all on the same side weren't we?

The contents of the tins were shared amongst the children who looked on the fruit with wonder as the train began to move on the final part of its journey now that the US stores train had gone. We had sated our appetites and been wondering what to do with the surplus fruit. Now the children would benefit. This had to be the most unusual 'pier-head' jump I had ever been involved in.

We were met by a lorry at Algiers and dumped our kit over the tail-gate and followed it inside for the short trip to the RN Base which would provide us with a much needed bath and food. I had set out with no 'draft chit', a half dozen sandwiches, travelled one night and two days in a cattle truck over 200 miles of single track railway along the North African coast and still I didn't know why! Next day I was escorted to a troopship to await passage back to Britain.

To digress just a little, the 12th Minesweeping Flotilla continued to do its good work in the Mediterranean for quite a while after I left it but I always felt a part of it and 60 years later am in touch with two shipmates from the *Acute*, John Pettigrew and Norman Chapman, who told me that after my sudden departure they went on to sweep for the landings at Sicily, Salerno, Anzio and the shipping lanes as far as Salonika in Greece. Perhaps a fitting end to this chapter is a quote from a report in the *Times of Malta* for Friday 5th April 1946:

12th MINESWEEPING FLOTILLA'S RECORD SCORE
Sterling Work in the Mediterranean
The famous Minesweeping Flotilla the 12th WS is shortly to return to England
After 3 years operational sweeping in the Mediterranean. During this time their 'bag' Has totalled 2715 (2715 mines

and 320 obstructions) and the Flotilla has swept the Allied Invading Forces into enemy-occupied ports from North Africa, Sicily, Salerno, and the whole West Coast of Italy. Their total score is the highest attained by an Mediterranean Flotilla. The "Twelfth" which now comprises the Algerine Class Fleet Minesweepers "Fly", "Acute", "Albacore" , "Cadmus", "Circe", "Esiegle", and "Mutine", with the Isle Class Danlayers "Helisay", "Hunda", "St.Kitts", "Fould" and "Kintyre", first arrived in the Mediterranean during the Invasion of North Africa in November 1942. They did sterling work in those early days, though not without loss, for "Algerine", the first "Senior Officer" of the Flotilla was torpedoed and sunk with heavy loss off Bougie, and the "Alarm" was bombed at Bone. Later, during clearance of the famous Tunisian War Channel "Fantome" had her stern blown off. Their places were taken by "Fly", and "Mutine" who came out from England to replace the casualties.

Always in Front

Throughout, the Twelfth has been in the forefront of all assaults. At Sicily, Salerno and Anzio they swept the assault forces into the beachhead. The Flotilla were the first Allied ships in Capri and had landed on the island even before Naples had fallen. Before Anzio they operated in the Gulf of Oacta while under fire from enemy shore batteries which swept along the line of sweepers and then, unaccountably, broke off the action once they had found the range! It was at the Gulf of Oacta too that the Twelfth did a particularly dangerous sweep at night which took them to within a half mile of the enemy coast.

ANZIO BEACHEAD

After the initial assault at Anzio with air battles overhead, the Flotilla continued to sweep off the beach head. During these operations "Circes" stern was blown off but she was repaired and later re-joined the Flotilla. Constantly hard on the heels of the Army and oft-times ahead, these sweepers were hard at work clearing channels to establish safe traffic lanes for Allied shipping. A marathon performance was the clearing of a two mile wide channel from Anzio to Leghorn, 90 miles long — a six week job which involved sweeping 234 square miles and clearing some 250 mines. On this operation they attracted the unwelcome attention of 'Leghorn Lizzie', a long range gun of at least 170 mm, cousin of 'Anzio Annie' whose acquaintance they had made earlier on!

Chapter 8

OVERLORD

On 15th October 1943 I was one of a draft of 50 ratings who sailed from Liverpool on the liner *Aquitania* bound for Boston, Massachusetts, U.S.A. This troopship was a former cruise liner now stripped down to serve her country and its wartime clientele. We were sailing as the result of the 'Lend-Lease Program' which Winston Churchill and President Roosevelt had worked out in Britain's most desperate days when America stood on the touch line discussing whether they should take over the Royal Navy as we succumbed to Hitler's plans to eliminate us. Instead Roosevelt decided to lease a batch of First World War Destroyers and that began the program of which we were now well and truly a part. America was now a part of the war and the ship we were to take over was brand new, one of a batch of many warships the US yards were building en masse.

Boston appeared on the horizon on 20th October and almost as soon as we docked we were put on a train which would take us to *USN Saker*, the navy yard which would be our temporary base. Saker was an accommodation centre where US and British crews were billeted as they waited for their ships to complete building and fitting out. Ours was to be one of a batch of 50 frigates destined to make a difference to the convoy escort and anti-submarine roles. The hotel, for that is what our accommodation was, could be described as luxurious after normal Royal Navy wartime standards. Bunks and proper food in large quantities were the order of the day and something we could get used to.

'Charlestown Naval Yard', where our ship was being built, was but one of several similar yards which included 'Asbury Park' near New York, 'Casco Bay', and 'Fargo Barracks'. Drafts could be sent to any of them.

I was at *Saker* from 21st October until 6th December 1943 when we commissioned *H.M.S. Kingsmill* and began acceptance trials in the yard before shake-down trials in Casco Bay. On 6th December we were ready to sail for the UK. Of all the escorts manned by the RN only two were built with a pre-planned destiny and they were *H.M.S. Lawford* and *Kingsmill*, which were to be Headquarters Ships for the planned Invasion of Europe. We would lie off the British beach in the 'Front Line'.

We, of course, did not know this at the time but we did have an idea something was definitely lined up for us because we did not do a normal work-up at Bermuda but set out for the UK straight away so that certain modifications could be carried out on the ship.

The Atlantic weather was foul as usual but we headed into it with great determination to follow orders so that being lashed and buffeted by high winds and heavy seas was not going to deter from getting home. Our first couple of days were the worst and we had no option but to ride them out before continuing our journey during which we had several asdic contacts which did not become positive. This was due as much to the weather as to crews lack of cohesion which itself was due to our not having worked up sufficiently. Time was at a premium!

Arriving back in the UK in mid-December we were sent at once to Cammell Lairds Yard in Liverpool so that work could begin on the ship to fit her for her coming role off 'Gold Beach'. The modifications were many, including an extra mast aft to hang the many radio and radar communication aerials we were going to need. Extra Oerlikon anti-aircraft guns – 16 of them – and very impressive they were. Our numbers also increased to over 220 by the addition of gunners, communication staff (W/T Operators and Radar Plotters) and, on the day before we sailed for France a number of Army Officers came aboard.

Alterations having been completed at Liverpool we were ordered to Belfast and Tobermory to fully work-up and shake-down which all went very well and we emerged as a fully ready fighting unit. We set off to sail down the coast to Weymouth and Portland to start a work-up and take part in exercises to fit us for our coming role about which we had not yet been officially told due to the need for secrecy. We knew it was in the coming Invasion, whenever that would be, but that is all.

At *H.M.S. Bee*, Weymouth, we berthed each evening after working to perfect our techniques during the day at sea. It was very busy, with the buildings alongside the wharf where we secured, having been converted to offices, and many different uniforms thronged the port, many of them American. Ships were also there in plenty.

One weekend I was lucky enough to secure two days off and took the opportunity to get home to Lymington where I found one of my brothers, an Engineer Lieutenant, RN, had also made it. It was such a long time since we had last seen each other. "Where are you based and what are you on?" he asked me and when I said *Kingsmill* at *H.M.S. Bee* in Weymouth his reply was, "Well, well, I am the Engineer Officer at *Bee* and I go on board *Kingsmill* most days when she is in harbour." We trooped off to the Angel Hotel and that night we also drank at the Mayflower Inn. From then on my brother almost always appeared on board *Kingsmill* at 'tot' time.

After all our trials and exercises in Studland Bay, Weymouth Bay, and off Portland we were ready for what was to come and at the end of May 1944 we sailed to Portsmouth to join our counterpart *H.M.S. Lawford* which was anchored in the Solent off Cowes. It seemed to us that whatever was planned for us could not be too far in the future.

H.M.S. Kingsmill

All leave was stopped at least a week before we were to do what the Admiralty had in store for the ship. For days we had watched the roads and spare ground at Gosport and Stokes Bay fill up with lorries, troops, and tanks and various other vehicles and bits of equipment, while tent cities had sprung up so that everything was bumper to bumper even on the grass verges. Ships also were constantly arriving and parking in long rows. On 1st June we were still anchored near the *Lawford* in atrocious weather. Rain and more rain fell but at least on board we had some respite. For the poor devils under canvas ashore it must have been miserable. After June 3rd things began happening, as boats filled with personnel, both Army and Navy were constantly arriving alongside and transferring them onto our ship and others. We embarked an extra 60 people so that on board were 180–240 men as the hour approached, This was as well as tons of extra stores and ammunition.

From 11 am on 5th June we knew that the word "GO" would be

said very soon. Everyone on tenterhooks but the bad weather never let up and the sea heaved until, at 10 pm it was "up anchor" and off we went. Ships in every direction around us were making their way towards the open sea. When we reached the English Channel it was a breathtaking sight there were so many vessels of all sorts ploughing towards - France. The horizon was thick with them. Even in the darkness we could feel them around us. Overhead the roar of aircraft added to the surreal scene. I was now a Leading Seaman SD (Submarine detector).

Having been 'fell out' from "special sea duty men" a small bunch of us tried to decide what exactly was going on, trying to make sense of the whole thing because as yet we had not been given the big picture. We could understand the need for secrecy and although we guessed that the Invasion was on we did not know where exactly was our destination.

If this was the Invasion of France then I was ready to record my thoughts, and so I settled down with some hot 'kai' one of the lads had brought and began to write a sequel to my poem "For Which They Wait" that I had penned three days earlier. I often wrote poems on board as a sort of diary in prose:

FOR WHICH THEY WAIT

A thousand craft at anchor lay, off Gurnard Bay,
A million men, and more, await the given word
When they shall move, as one, toward their goal,
Determined in purpose – a prayer in every soul,
Waiting, ever waiting, 'till the signal 'Go' is heard
Then shall a thousand cannons roar
Aye, and a thousand more!

Then shall the darkness be as light,
Our quest for right
From end to end, gun flashes mark the coast

And bursts of fire explode with thunder in the sky,
When German planes 'tis thought were passing by
That once with pride, the arrogant did boast,
Shall be met in combat, Hun!
When we come!

Then shall be seen the outcome of it all,
When they fall –
Let's get it over soon, let us be gone
Confident in Faith to meet what waits
Across the ditch – from Lands End to the Straits
A thousand ships will soon sail proudly on –
And history itself will then be made
When we invade!

Meanwhile we wait 'till they that know
Shall say 'GO!'
A thousand ships are loaded for that day
Armed, provisioned, filled with men that know
They too shall share the mighty 'Victory' blow
When the word is said – 'BE ON YOUR WAY'!
Then shall a thousand cannon roar –
Aye, and a thousand more!

5th June 1944

So now the order 'GO' has been said and here we are steaming for
France. My thoughts are mixed and confused. Are we going to be
blasted back into the sea – whatever happens it is sure that many of
those among this mighty armada will not return from this venture.
So then I will give my nerves a boost and sit and pen some lines of
comfort:

The VICTORY POEM

The Day has come on which we stake our all.
Mighty Allied Nations will rise, or bravely fall,
Soldiers, Sailors, Airmen, eager in full array
Onward into battle, for this one is OUR Day!

Kingsmills, hold your rush,
Your job has been well planned,
Elevate your guns and keep them ready manned,
For what goes up must come down,
You know as well as I,
Jerry's boasted 'Luftwaffe'
You can blast from out the sky!

A million prayers are not too many if they are
truly meant.
In battle Faith is high – and many lives are spent.
But they are freely offered – for Victory is the prize
Their memory treasured ever – it lives and never dies.

Think only of one thing when battles roar begins,
Complete destruction only to the Nazi's and their sins,
Don't stay your hand through conscience – qualms or
Any way defer
The best that is within you – death to defeat, prefer!

For what lies now before us, let us be well prepared,
Steal your mind and nerves and hand, let careless shots
Be spared.
As we enter into battle and give what's long been due –
May God be ever with us, NOW BOYS, ITS UP TO YOU!

6th June 1944

It will not be long now before all kinds of things will begin to happen so I find a suitable position on the upper deck from where I can watch the outcome of this massive exercise. I have no particular duty to perform until such times as we are in position, as near to where it was decided to drop anchor and proceed to carry out our duties as Headquarters ship for Gold Beach, off Aromanches. As dawn broke one began to get a picture of what we were about. All hell broke loose – the large gun emplacements the Germans had built with slave labour high above the beaches were firing into our invading armada and our ships in turn were ferociously replying as our warships and rocket projectile barges let go their explosives. Above, the R.A.F. were continuously bombing the beaches and emplacements as well as the area behind the beaches.

So many things were happening in the light of the new day that it is not possible to recount even all that one saw, there are only impressions. By 8.30am we were anchored in position. As I looked towards Gold Beach all seemed total chaos. The noise was deafening, gunfire, rifle fire, shouts, screams, shells exploding. *H.M.S. Lawford* was anchored nearby with Captain Pugsley on board, who was in charge of the anchorage defence and of the Coastal Forces frigates which were operating further out to deal with any E boats which might be tempted to interfere.

My particular job now was to work with an Officer-In-Charge of a reception party which is perhaps a suitable term for the activity. Our task was on the starboard quarter of the quarter deck where a steady flow of landing craft were to be received and from them the many wounded were to be unloaded into the care of Medical Officers and Sick Berth Attendants who would give immediate first aid to stabilise wounds. After that first aid they were carried to the port quarter where empty landing craft were waiting to transport them to hospital ships anchored further off shore.

Normal routines like 'hands to dinner' or 'fall in port watch' were of no relevance here as everyone got on with whatever jobs they were assigned to. I watched as the first landing craft approached the beach, first passing close by our side their soldiers fully laden with packs and weapons, standing shoulder to shoulder as the craft plunged onwards to their destiny, tossed about by waves. There would be an occasional eruption as a mine exploded under or near a landing craft just as the ramps splashed down as they beached. The whole contents of the craft would be flung into the air. Whole groups of soldiers ballooned aloft and splashed down into the sea. Mixed in with that were explosions from shells fired by the enemy, the many warships, and bombs dropping from our aircraft.

By noon, through to late afternoon I and my party of sailors were kept busy. It was no mean task to get the wounded aboard and to load them into landing craft afterwards for their journey inwards to safety. Some men had limbs blown off or had severe internal injuries or head wounds. We had to be as gentle as possible yet be firm and steel ourselves to our task, as they had earlier. It was heartbreaking work to deal with so much pain and misery.

I recall one boat coming alongside and among the wounded as I peered inside, was a soldier, among many others who had parachuted into his war and been raked by enemy machine-gun fire. His right a rm and left thigh were shot through. Meanwhile all our extra staff, the W/T operat o rs and radar operators, and Staff Officers continued to cope with their tasks despite the blood and gore around them. We were very thankful - that we were afloat and not on shore.

By dawn of D-Day + 1 it was known that our troops had done well ashore and a foothold had been established with prospects for greater advances this day. What we found most poignant was the number of bodies floating past us as we did our work, some face down, others face up. All had heavy packs on and I wondered where they would go as they were swept aside by the coming and going of the landing craft. Were they recovered by boats?

A couple of days on and vehicles, tanks, stores and men, were already pouring ashore without resistance as the advance continued. *H.M.S. Kingsmill*'s job, as with *H.M.S. Lawford* was to maintain order on the beach area and there were many alarms during that first day, and the one after.

The Germans had used several types of attack. Often our sea boat was lowered and as its coxswain I would cruise around in it looking for enemy manned torpedo's among our ships. The pilots of these craft sat in a cockpit on the torpedo and he would aim it at a suitable ship and attack, losing his life in the process. I never did see one though. Another weapon was a motor boat, the bows filled with

H.M.S. Kingsmill, HQ ship for 'Gold Beach'. We are the two-masted ship behind the Oerlikon gun. June 6th 1944

explosive although in this case the pilot would aim his craft and jump out before it crashed into its target. There were plenty of scares to keep us on our toes and that included German aircraft attacks. A few of their dive bombers and fighters got through the air screen and then *Kingsmill's* Oerlikons, and everyone else's, come to that, would open up. A Ju88 which headed over the fleet brought a most impressive response from all guns. It burst into flames and crashed into the sea.

We seldom left our anchorage but our sister ship did, especially when E boats were reported to be about. In the early morning, shortly after the 6th, *H.M.S.Lawford* had returned to our anchorage after one of these forays and was preparing to let go her hook when an enemy bomber appeared and dived on her, loosing two bombs which were direct hits and she sank in a very short time.

Our activities continued until the beach activities became more settled, after about five days. The next morning was piped "shore leave to 1st part of port watch from 1200 hours to 1600 hours". This was out of the blue and as I was port watch I decided to take the opportunity.

A landing craft picked 16 of us up and put us down on Gold Beach in full shore going rig as though we were in Pompey. We were warned to be ready for departure on the dot or we would be classed as adrift. Taking different tracks across the sand our soldiers had fought and died for, and up the slopes they had won, till we reached the road at the top. It was all much like the English countryside with green fields stretching into the distance but, curiously, there was not a soul about. I was on my own so l turned right. Without a clue as to where I was or where I was going it felt so strange, but also peaceful after the hectic pace of the last few days.

I was walking along on the grass verge when I heard shouting and saw a couple of British 'Tommies' in the road ahead, both waving their arms about. As I got nearer I saw they were in full fighting rig, grenades and rifles slung about them. They looked at me curiously. "What the bloody hell are you doing here Jack, dressed up like a fairy (in my best bib and tucker) and where do you think you are going anyway – have you got any identification on you?" I produced my 'I/D' and after studying it they both told me to keep off the verges as they could be mined. I continued my stroll, enjoying the peace and quiet and surreal solitude until noticing an avenue of trees to my right with a grass track in the middle. This will do to exercise a bodily function which was needing a solution, I thought. Thirty yards in seemed suitable. There was a ditch on either side, topped with long grass. In proceeding to relieve myself in one ditch I detected a tinny sound and so moved across to the other side of the ditch where I heard it again. Getting hold of a small branch I poked aside the long grass and saw a cache of land mines each about 18 inches across. I checked the other ditch and amongst more mines I came across a cache of hand grenades and picked one up.

H.M.S. Glasgow – a previous ship – receiving a direct-hit from the shore batteries on D-day, 6th June 1944.

I was curious because they were all chromium plated, lovely and shiny, unlike our normal green ones. These were German 'stick grenades' so called because they were thrown by holding the stick to which they were attached.

What a splendid keepsake I thought to myself so I stuck one down the front of my jumper and made my way back to the road and continued on. It was not long before a dispatch rider slowed down behind me, I think he probably had a chat with the two soldiers I had met, because he was quite friendly and interested in my plans.

He was riding a 350cc Royal Enfield with girder forks and tubular steel pannier-rack behind his seat. "Where are you headed Jack?" he asked me and when I said I hadn't a clue he told me he was going to Bayeux with signals so "if you fancy a trip you can come with me and I will drop you at the top of Gold Beach on my return."

That was fine with me and I climbed aboard. We rattled on for about nine miles or so and as we bumped up and down I became somewhat curious as to how a grenade stuffed down my front would behave in such circumstances, and played safe by heaving it into a nearby hedge as we passed by. Entering the outskirts of Bayeux my pal turned his head to me and told me to "keep yer head down Jack, there's snipers around here."

We went a fair bit down a main road and stopped at a building on the left, like a town hall with large stone pillars in front. "You had better come with me and shelter behind a pillar while I deliver these signals", said my friend. His task done we headed back to Arromanches and I arrived back with plenty of time to catch the boat to my ship. Only recently when contacting a former member of *Kingsmills* company did I find that he and two others of the shore party had gone on the same route but got a lift in an Army jeep to Caen, also returning to the beach in time.

Chapter 9

I JOIN UP AGAIN

At the end of WWII my rating was Leading Seaman and my ship was *H.M.S. Brissenden.* Having by now passed professionally for Petty Officer it transpired that it was that ship I was rated up to Petty Officer.

My next draft was to *H.M.S. Collingwood* as ship's company where I was made P. O. of the main gate for a while. From there I went to the M.T.B. Base in Gosport, *H.M.S. Hornet*, as Coxswain of MTB 5003. Later on I was recalled to *H.M.S.Victory* and informed that my non-substantive rate as a Submarine Detector was no longer appropriate, and I should request to qualify for a different non-sub rating. After a lot of thought I requested to change to the Fleet Air Arm as a P. O. Aircraft Handler (PO/AH).

On 25th September 1947 I joined *H.M.S. Siskin* at Gosport, the former R.A.F. Gosport Coastal Command base, now known as *H.M.S Sultan.* My course began. At that time *Siskin* still had its grass runways, but set into the tarmac area was a dummy aircraft carrier deck where the practical training was carried out in conjunction with nearby F.A.A. Station *H.M.S. Deadalus.* We learned parking procedures, take-off and landing signals for use at sea, aircraft crash and fire rescue techniques. The qualifying exams were taken at *Daedalus.*

Having qualified as as a PO (Air) Aircraft Handler I joined *H.M.S. Condor,* then a naval air station at Arbroath, Scotland. There I took over as Petty Officer in charge of the Fire & Rescue Station situated inside, to the left of, the main gate. We had a crew of eight plus

Crash & Fire Crew, H.M.S. Condor, Arbroath, Scotland

myself to work a domestic fire appliance, simply a fully equipped fire engine which was used to deal with ordinary house fires. There was also an ambulance and two large Ford Crash Tenders for the airfields use when flying was in progress. The tenders were well used as flying was mainly done with torpedo carrying 'Barracudas' which were rather ungainly types said to have been designed by committee.

They used to drop torpedoes at old naval ships no longer in commission and going to the breakers yard in tow but unmanned. I did that job whilst I was at Condor where we had our share of crashes and rescues. Two occasions stand out for me, both involving single crew aircraft where the pilot was shunted forward, hitting his head and being rendered unconscious at the same time as the machine burst into flames. We were always ready and on full alert alongside the control tower but on such occasions by the time we reached the crash scene there was no hope of rescuing the pilots. Sometimes there would be no fire to deal with so the aircrew and passengers were rescued.

During the following months I enjoyed a steady run of normal day to day activities in the department which included civilian and service fire and rescue work. In off duty hours we were occasionally called in to back up the local civilian fire service in Arbroath. In those days they were part-timers whereas we were on 24 hour call-out.

Being single and a native of the South Coast of England stuck so far north was no problem for me but a problem which was looming on the near horizon concerned my 12 years engagement being up. I had to make up my mind whether or not to sign on for another 10 years and thus earn my pension, or perhaps I would be better off getting back into 'civvie street'.

Luckily a solution presented itself in a most unexpected way. One of the pilots stationed at *Condor* was a Lieutenant Luther with whom I was on close chatting terms. My office was at the rear of the fire station and sometimes he would pop in for a chat as I was there on most working days. On one occasion we were having our usual talk about life when he said to me "Your time must soon be up Ron, have you thought about signing on?" I replied that "Frankly I am undecided what to do for the best having no idea what is outside. "He said, "I'll tell you why I asked. Shortly I am going down to London, to the Air Ministry and if you wish I will ask them what civilian jobs they have which might interest you. Perhaps they could offer you a job straight away. Your dilemma would be made somewhat easier." I thanked him and promptly forgot about it all until some 10 days later in came the Lieutenant to tell me his few words at the Air Ministry, and they did indeed have a vacancy which would be ideal for me. It was working for the Ministry of Civil Aviation at Dyce Airport near Aberdeen where I would be part of the Fire & Rescue crew. I gathered that they would jump at the chance of taking of a fully trained man. Lt. Luther assured me that the Airport Manager would be contacting me to offer an interview. He also asked me to give it some thought as "you have run this department efficiently for 14 months and they really want you, so don't dismiss the idea too soon."

A week later a telephone call came for me from the Airport Manager, during which we discussed a few points and he asked me to go and see him which a few days later I did. I pointed out that there were two problems which might prevent me taking the post, were it to be offered. The Airport was isolated, some four or more miles from town and finding accommodation would be a problem. I also had two months to serve in the Royal Navy and so could not take the job right away. "Is that all?" he said. "Well I think I can solve both problems for you. Take as long as you like to join us because the crew can go on overtime to cover the vacancy and they won't object to that. As far as the other point is concerned we have a contingent of the R.A.F. stationed here with their Spitfires and other reserve aircraft. As well as being airport manager I am also a retired Group Captain, and I am sure I can sort out accommodation for you. I will arrange for you to become an honorary member of the Sergeants' Mess, as befits your Petty Officer rank, and so you will have a cabin to yourself and free use of the facilities! Now Mr Walsh, give this proposal careful thought and call me in a day or so to let me know what you have decided. I have been strongly advised by London to get you here if I can, so I hope that your answer will be yes."

I put in my request to leave the navy on completion of my time. *H.M.S. Condor* immediately relieved me of my duties and on 8th April 1949 I reported to *H.M.S. Daedalus* at Lee-on-Solent for discharge from the Royal Navy – Time Served!

As a Petty Officer (Air) PERM, I was released into the reserve on 14th May (extended time expired) and a week later travelled from my home in Lymington as a civilian, to Dyce Airport, Scotland and reported for duty as a member of the Ministry of Civil Aviation Authority's Crash & Tender Crew.

The crash crew of 12 men, all except me, lived in Aberdeen whereas I had the promised cabin at the R.A.F. Sergeants' Mess with full use of their facilities which I greatly appreciated especially as the airport was a flying duties only field with no 24 hour facilities which could be pretty boring. Actual flying hours were 8am to 6pm. Should an aircraft be in difficulties the tower would alert us and we went on immediate standby while the pilot began to circle the airfield in order to use up fuel, which lessened the landing weight and also cut down the chance of it burning if it crashed. Our Fordson crash tenders had a crash bar across the front which enabled us to push down any five-barred gates on farmers' fields to get to crash site which were well away from the airfield. Permission to do so had been given by local farmers, who would receive due recompense for any damage to gates or crops.

Six Spitfires were flown by the Royal Air Force Reserve on training flights from Dyce. Numbered among the pilots was a member of our crash crew who had flown them in wartime, and off watch from his crash duties he could often be found in the air above the airport. Towards the end of my time at Dyce there was an unfortunate incident. The airport manager had flown to Turnhouse Airport, Edinburgh, to attend a weekend conference and had accepted a lift back in an aircraft which left before his own scheduled flight. I remember the morning very well being on duty when I was informed that the Group Captain's aircraft was overdue. By noon concern was mounting as no information had reached us as to any emergency landing having taken place due to bad weather or mechanical trouble. Then a phone call to 'Mitch' our Spitfire pilot asked for him to take a Spitfire up and overfly the route which should have been used. The outcome was tragic for everyone as he spotted wreckage on the side of a mountain when investigated by ground rescue services turned out to be our missing aircraft. All on board were dead.

Ministry of Civil Aviation (M.C.A.) Dyce Airport, Aberdeen
Fire and Crash Crew (I am third from the right, front row)

Loneliness during off-duty hours was a factor which I found to be something I was not used to and nor did I like it. So after making a few phone calls to Aberdeen I traced what I was looking for and off I went by bus returning with a three month old alsatian puppy, a pedigree, who settled down in my quarters quickly and within a couple of weeks was a welcome member of Dyce crash crew. The lads spoilt him during duty hours and when the airfield was closed we had miles of space to exercise in. I registered him with the Kennel Club and named him 'Prince of Dyce'. He answered to 'Prince' of course. His favourite place was in the cab with me except when we had a call-out or training excise when he would remain in the crew room.

One thing I could never get used to was^ when the lads went on strike for two or three days over some grievance or other and did not come into work. On such occasions I had to sit it out, unpaid, until they decided to return to work. Over the months 'Prince' turned into a lovely dog in every way and I joined the Aberdeen alsatian Club so that at weekends we were able to give obedience exhibitions at public grounds which gave him the opportunity to earn himself a variety of medals. In the winter months when it snowed, and we certainly got our share of it in Scotland. Prince could not get enough of it, wanting to be up and out as soon as he was awake each day. The pleasure he got, and imparted to me as he ran and dived, rolled in it and barked at it, was a joy. One of the crews tasks was to snow plough the runways and sweeping the perimeters tracks and hard- standings all day to keep the field open and paying its way. I found it necessary but monotonous. 'Prince' loved every minute of it especially sitting in the cab.

With the advent of Spring I began to seriously look to my future, feeling that I really did not want another winter like the one just past. By then I was a Leading Fireman and I decided to transfer to an air station down South, preferably in Hampshire, and so I put in my request. I explained the reasons to the new airport manager and he was quite understanding, saying he would forward my request along with his own recommendations to head office. A week later a draft to Hurn Airport came through. Bournemouth's Hurn Airport, or Christchurch as it also was known, was not far from Lymington which meant it was most suitable for seeing my family. I left behind

Prince at Dyce Airport (M.C.A.)

some very good friends at Dyce but it was a wise move on my part.

Hurn Airport was then in a semi-desolate area but was nothing like Dyce, and anyway I had living accommodation in an MOD building on the outskirts of the airfield. I had brought 'Prince' down with me but left him with my parents at Lymington until I sorted myself out. He settled down superbly with them which was just as well because it was made clear to me that a dog could not be kept at the airfield. That was just one of the needless niggles which the authority brought up but others were to surface later and they would cloud the pleasure I felt at being in home surroundings once more.

The crash crew was larger at Hurn than at Dyce and everyone was in work by 7.30am and away by 5pm, so I had little chance to get to know them other than during manning of the vehicles or on exercises. As at Dyce there was a practice of striking every so often for more pay and better conditions which left me isolated and losing pay as well as being on my own for however long it took for them to return.

I took a bike ride to my home at such times as it was always good to see my folks and Prince. For about six months I cycled home at every opportunity. When I had a few days leave I took the opportunity to seek my fathers advice. All along he had thought I was unwise to leave the navy and his advice to me was to see if it was possible to rejoin and complete my 22 years for a pension.

Going to the Navy recruiting office in Southampton I passed the necessary tests and was asked to return in two days. I did so and a Commander informed me that I could not get back in as a Fleet Air Arm P0 (Air) - but they could accept me as a Seaman Petty Officer as I had previously been one. That suited me fine and a week later, having handed in my notice at Hurn I re-joined at *H.M.S. Victory Barracks* in Portsmouth on 3rd March 1952, firstly as an Able Seaman, on 4th March as a Leading Seaman, and on 5th March as a Petty Officer (Permanent). I was back again in the navy!

Prince on H.M.S. 1801

For a month I enjoyed a 'quiet number' as a staff car driver ferrying officers to and from places of duty locally and also to and from London and various towns and airports.

All good things come to an end and my staff car driving certainly did when I got a draft note and request to report to the drafting office where I was told where I was off to and also informed that my Divisional Officer would like to see me before I left Victory. I went to see him and he said, "We are sending you on this draft mainly to see what the outcome will be. Up until now the Commanding Officer (of the ship) has been dissatisfied with every Coxswain we have sent to him, putting in requests for new ones at regular intervals. The size of the ship is ideal for an acting PO to be Coxswain and gain experience of the job in a sea going berth. However", he continued, "you are to replace the acting PO Coxswain he has at present." My draft was to *H.M.S. 1801,* near Edinburgh.

She's a small ship whose crew numbered 12 which included the CO, a Lieutenant, and 'Jimmy' also a Lieutenant. I was in charge of the crew under the 'Jimmy' whilst a Stoker PO ran the engine room. After a long rail journey I was met by the man I was relieving who took me down to my cabin which was shared by the Stoker PO. The disembarking Cox'n had no intention of lingering, he was already packed ready to go. He gave me the CO's instructions which were that once I had relieved him he was to report to the CO in the Wardroom and then leave the ship for his next draft. He said he had dreaded every day since joining *1801*. "You will understand when you meet the Captain," he said.

I unpacked and made up my bunk, had a chat with Ted Blake, my cabin mate, before going to the Wardroom myself to report myself officially on board. The CO said "You are welcome on board my ship Coxswain and I will see you in the Wardroom at 10am tomorrow morning to let you know what I expect of you."

Later on Ted and I had a wander to the Senior Rates Mess to pass away the evening and get to know one another. I learnt much from Ted. Apparently this CO expected 'Big Ship' routine and the obvious one to make that happen was the Cox'n. He had seen two A/PO Coxswains come and go in short order and both could not get off the ship fast enough. Our base was *H.M.S. Lochinvar*, near Edinburgh.

At 10am I presented myself in the Wardroom in my best uniform where the Captain and 1st Lt.' waited for me. The Captain then said, "I am pleased to meet you and you are obviously an experienced three badge Petty Officer with a row of medals to prove it, and I feel we will get on well together in the future. I require big ship routine worked on board *1801*, regardless of our being in harbour or at sea. Anyone seen smoking on the upper deck or out of rig-of-the-day is to be put on report. And if my orders are strictly carried out then I am sure we will have an efficient ship. Our duties are many and varied and we spend a lot of time at sea doing patrols and escort duties, dan laying, exercises, etc." He then asked me, "Are you happy with that Coxswain?" I told him yes and rejoined Ted in the cabin.

We remained in harbour for the next few days which enabled me to settle in and meet the ship's company, where they worked and what their duties were. I felt that my time on board could prove to be happy. After a couple of weeks all was seemingly running smoothly. We spent a lot more time at sea, often leaving harbour at 9am and sometimes not returning until late evening. I had got used to the now familiar 'pipe' over the ship's tannoy, "Coxswain on the bridge." When I arrived the CO would say something like "Cox 'n, Able Seaman Scott has just come on deck improperly dressed without cap and I want him on my report." We always had a number of men on report and under punishment 'doing their bit' after working hours.

Ted and I spent a lot of hours during our evening free time sitting in the mess just across from the ship's berth. Apart from Lochinvar it was the base for several 'Ton' class minesweepers, and while relaxing over a pint we would meet with 'old ships' chums from ships we had served on and whom we had not seen for a while recounting runs ashore or events of interest that happened in the past.

One day I received a letter from my dad at home in Lymington that caused me much anxiety. Both dad and mum were now elderly and on their own at home, and dad told me that my dog 'Prince' was not at all happy being parted from his master, and what could I do about it. I wrote out a request for 'permission to keep a dog on board' and put it through channels. The CO duly sent for me and when I reported to the Wardroom he and his First Lieutenant listened to my explanation as I told them about having Prince as a pup, him being with me for so long, and how I had re-entered the navy and had to farm him out at home and now my parents were elderly. I gave them the full story. To my surprise the Captain and First agreed that providing I could cope with the situation I could have Prince on board on a trial basis of two weeks.

If all went well then that time would be extended. You can imagine my delight as I motored down to Lymington and after a weekend at home headed back to the ship with Prince by my side. Good lad that he was he accepted his new life very well considering what he had to learn, including negotiating the ladder to my cabin which, with Ted and I and now Prince in it was pressed for breathing space.

Prince had a nice warm carpet to sleep on and he soon got his sea legs. It was not unknown when we were in harbour, and the Captain was entertaining guests for him to send a messenger who would tell me that he would like Prince in the Wardroom to join the party. The CO and 1st Lt. also often liked to have Prince for company and he did not mind at all for I guess he enjoyed extra treats. Anyway, Prince soon became a firm favourite on board and friend to all as well as being looked after by everyone.

Life on board progressed and went on like this for most of a year or so until I began to detect a distinct change in the CO's attitude, mainly towards me. It seemed that he was not happy that I went ashore as often as I could when we were in harbour and off duty. He made it plain that two nights each week were plenty. This did not add up or seem reasonable to me, after all I was only a few yards away from the ship in the base Senior Rate's Mess. A phone call would get me if I was needed!

I continued as normal and assumed after a few weeks that life on a small ship with a big ship routine was being enjoyed by all once again, However, this was not so as the CO convinced the First Lieutenant that I was neglecting my duties by not being on board at every opportunity, or as much as he thought I should be. Unaware of this simmering away in the background I was rather surprised one morning when, we having secured alongside the jetty in port, a messenger brought me a request to go to the Wardroom. At first it all seemed pleasant enough when I got there, until the CO came right out with it. "Cox 'n," he began, "I think it only fair to tell you that I must get rid of you, and therefore I am warning you of that fact. Is there anything you would like to say about it?" I replied with a non-committal "No, Sir", whereupon he dismissed me.

When I returned to my cabin I discussed this with Ted and we concluded that there was little that could be done about it other than await the outcome. The pair of Lieutenants, CO and First, had obviously worked out some plan of action that would cause me to be on my way without them having to apply to 'drafters' for a replacement Coxswain.

Their scheme came together a few weeks later when we had been at sea for a day exercise and had returned to Port Edgar that night. I had been on the wheel as we went under the Forth Bridge and then came close into the jetty where we dropped anchor instead of going alongside and securing as we normally did. It was most unusual and I should have been warned, but I assumed it was to get an early start in the morning, though I would have expected that I would be informed about this departure from custom.

"Special sea duty men" had fallen out and Ted and I were about to turn-in for the night. It was about midnight when we put out the lights and went to sleep.

A messenger entered the cabin and went to wake Ted who slept in the top bunk, and I heard him say that Ted was to go to the engine-room and immediately close-up, on CO's orders. As there was no further instruction I assumed this did not concern me (though as Cox'n it should have done), and I dozed off again until alerted by the engines starting and the cable beginning to crank back up into the ships hawse pipe. I glanced at my watch in the cabin light – it was 15 minutes past midnight, so with no orders to the contrary I just lay there and awaited developments.

When the anchor was up and felt the ship underway I knew there was something very wrong going on. We could only have moved a few hundred yards when the cable was let go again after which the ship came to a halt. Ted came back down to the cabin and asked me what that was all about. I told him that I had a feeling there would be developments to come and they would involve me. I was not

121

wrong! Having just dozed off once again the messenger arrived and this time he had the CO's order for me to attend him on the bridge right away. When I presented myself the CO and First Lieutenant were waiting and this latter Officer placed me in front of the Captain and said. "Off caps." I removed my head gear and he said, "You are on CO's report as having been absent from your place of duty at 23.50 hours, namely, at the wheel when the ship moved position." The CO then said, "You are on the Captain of *H.M.S. Lochinvar* report for being absent from place of duty. You will accompany me to *H.M.S. Lochinvar* after we have berthed alongside in the morning."

At 9am the next morning I was at the Captain of Lochinvar's defaulters table being charged with "being absent", and when asked for my comments I told him that the messenger, when I asked him if the Captain ordered that I , as well as the Stoker PO, should go to my place of duty as Coxswain, for moving ship, had replied, No! Then I said that "special sea duty men to close up" had not been piped either. The Captain of Lochinvar told me to "stand over." I was dismissed until a further hearing.

Ted and I went across to the Senior rates Mess for the next few evenings, and during that period I discovered from the base secretarial staff that the case was causing a fair amount of activity between the staff and RNB Portsmouth. Four days later I was told to report to the hearing room next day at 9am where the original charge was read out again, followed by Lochinvar's Captain saying "Case dismissed!"

I went back to my ship to resume my duties and await their outcome. Next day I was told to pack and was given a draft chit to RNB Portsmouth. It would appear that the CO of the ship, and his 1st. Lt. were also sent on draft and presumably *H.M.S. 1801* went to sea with a new Captain, First Lieutenant and Coxswain.

My time from February until October 1953 was spent on *H.M.S.*

Charity and *H.M.S. Creole* as 'stand by buffer' during both ships' refits, after which I returned to Portsmouth and was drafted to *H.M.S. Boxer*, a strange looking ship which had originally been a tank landing ship (US). She had been built upwards on the upper deck by introducing class rooms for training classes from *H.M.S. Dryad* and *H.M.S. Mercury*, (both bases now moved to *H.M.S. Collingwood*) which were Signals and Wireless Telegraphy (WT) shore training bases to the rear of Portsdown Hill. To add further to her unique appearance four masts were situated along her upper deck to facilitate the use of the signals and wireless instruction.

We mostly took classes to sea and cruised about all day in the area of the Nab Tower. We certainly got about a bit during the 22 months I was on board. One of our regular visits was to the River Dart at Dartmouth, Devon, where the Royal Britannia Officers training college was situated.

When I left *Boxer* in 1955 I reported to Pompey Barracks once more and within a few days was off to Hong Kong to join Motor Launch 3512 as her Cox'n. She was based with the Hong Kong Flotilla. I had read in the national newspapers at the time I received the draft chit, that an ML of that Flotilla had been fired upon when undertaking a routine patrol and most of the crew, including her captain had been killed. I guessed that my new post would be an interesting one.

Chapter 10

HONG KONG FLOTILLA

The troopship having left Liverpool with its usual load of men and women of all three services, including some families, all bound for a variety of posts abroad, took six weeks to get me to my station which I arrived at early in 1955. Although a long one the trip was interesting and as well as a good mix on board there were also several bars and plenty of upper deck to lounge about on in deck chairs. Small groups would gather in the evenings or we would mix with the families joining their husbands on accompanied tours. Among the Passengers was Bill Speakman VC, with his wife, off to Hong Kong for a spell of duty. Bill had won his Victoria Cross during the Korean War. I found him to be a most pleasant man, very sociable, and I got to know him quite well on the trip.

At Hong Kong those of us joining the ML's were homed in the shore base *H.M.S. Tamar* until taking over duties on board our boats. Married men, most of them, had their families there and lived ashore when not out on patrol. I was victualled by, and lived in, the PO's Mess at *Tamar*. My good chum Petty Officer Jim O'Neill, who had travelled out with me was taking over as Cox'n of *H.M. M.L. 3511*. He eventually got his wife Bridie and son out with him so that I lost my shore going 'oppo' from then on.

The job mainly consisted of patrol work around Hong Kong and its adjacent waters, one boat always out patrolling to intercept and board any suspect junks which may be smuggling people or drugs. There were even pirates to combat who were a real menace. Because the mainland of China was held by Chinese Communists we were instructed never to enter the Pearl River or any of their territorial waters. Each patrol was of three days duration with three days in harbour, or as we were needed, depending on the patrol register. Patrols were quite straight forward and often even quite pleasant if the weather was clement and mostly it was sunny and hot. We had an open bridge with, usually, myself at the wheel and the C.O., Lieutenant Stewart, RN, beside me.

It did not take long before I had a car and a part-time job with the Tombola Committee of the China Fleet Club. This was ideal because my off-patrol time could be filled with an interesting and lucrative occupation. Tombola was a very popular event at the Club not only for the service personnel but also large numbers of civilian businessmen and families. Sessions were a real social occasion.

I had been in Hong Kong a few weeks when I decided to take a ferry across the harbour to Kowloon. I strolled around the streets and came upon some local lads poking sticks through the bars of a cage outside a pet shop. Inside it was a monkey who was very unhappy by the sound of him. When I bent down to peer inside at the poor little fellow he gnashed his teeth and generally made it plain he was angry which he had every right to be.

The owner was out of his shop in a flash as he spotted a potential buyer. "You want buy?" I told him I was just looking but he insisted I come into his shop where he had more interesting items for purchase. These were a large and sorry looking brown bear and a couple of pythons, but I began to make my way back to the street with him on my heels. "You buy monkey then?" I agreed that I would and he packed the 'monk' in a large box which I carried back to the ferry. The poor creature was most upset and banged on his box and screamed defiance. When we reached *Tamar* I made up a box-cage more suitable for a small monkey to sleep in. It had wire at the front so that he could see out and he certainly would not be poked by small boys in his new life. I set him up in the balcony outside my bed space in the PO's Mess. The balcony overlooked a busy road into Hong Kong centre and we fellow occupants of the mess

The monkey, 'Monk', I had at H.M.S. Tamar, Hong Kong, 1956

spent many pleasant hours sitting in a group on the balcony, chatting and watching the world go by below us.

A couple of weeks and 'Monks' behaviour had improved. He had a comfy cage, and friendly faces around him with tasty tid-bits and no cruelty. I now applied to keep a monkey on board and my request was granted so 'Monk' was now official. My next purchase was of a dogs collar and long lead so now I was able to take him for a run ashore when we both needed a break. The collar fitted around his narrow waist and he used to run ahead of me just as a dog would until he spotted a dog or something of which he was frightened. That would bring him running back and up my shins to sit on my shoulder until the coast was clear when he would scamper off again. He was a pest in the car, a little Hillman Imp. His habit was to sit on the top of the bench seat staring at what was happening ahead. Now driving in the centre of Hong Kong was always fraught with danger and levels of anxiety were high, but in my case they were higher due to 'Monks' habit of suddenly leaping down from his perch. Quick as a flash jumping up from the seat to switch off the ignition which he had seen me do. Immediately coming to a sudden halt nose-to-tail in heavy traffic there would occur a fanfare of frantic car horns and impolite gestures and screaming from fellow road users. I would dart for the ignition and pray that the engine would start first go.

When it was 3512's turn to go out on patrol there was always a willing volunteer to keep an eye on 'Monk' until my return. Life went smoothly on a very pleasant job consisting of a few days on patrol, a few days on *Tamar*, a trip or two to the beach with Jim and his wife and son and, of course, 'Monk'. Things settled down to a routine so one day on patrol I felt sufficiently happy to speak to the CO, who was standing alongside me, about bringing 'Monk' on our next patrol but he was not all that keen on the idea. He felt it might cause all sorts of problems with a monkey running loose around the boat. I well appreciated his concerns but told him I had to get 'Monk' trained up a lot more and that I could then keep him well under control. A short trial period was agreed to and so on our very next

'Monk' on M.L. 3512

patrol the boat signed on a new crew member, Seaman Monk!

'Monk' used to sit in front of me when I was at the wheel, until we were clear of the harbour and I was relieved for a while. I would then walk him around the upper deck until he found for himself a favourite place, on the stern guard rail, beside the ensign staff which he could hold on to if we hit a spot of 'roughers'. He spent a lot of time up there secured by his collar and lead to prevent his loss overboard. With the CO beside me we were able to look around every so often to make sure he was still there.

At the end of the day when we anchored for the night, we would retire to my cabin which was shared with Ernie Hodgkins, the Stoker PO in charge of the engine room. After making up my books and when it was time to turn in, I would click my fingers and Monk would lay flat on his back, legs in the air, so that I could put on his specially adapted nappy. It had a hole cut in it so I could get his long tail through then cross it over in front and secure it with a safety pin. Then it was into my bunk with 'Monk' 'crashed out' beside me. When we returned to Hong Kong we easily slipped back into PO's Mess routine.

Towards the end of my time in Hong Kong there occurred an incident. I was not available in Tamar for most of the evening, being on duty in the China Fleet Club as a member of the Committee I didn't return to the Mess until around midnight. That evening there had been a dance in the C.P.O.'s Mess which was below our Mess. During breaks in the dancing groups of Chiefs and their wives were discussing various - topics when the subject of 'Monk' came up and some of the ladies were anxious to see *Tamar*'s monkey. One Chief decided to make it possible for them to see him and went to the balcony where he was kept in his cage which I kept locked at all times. This Chief asked several of my Mess mates where I kept the key and they told him it was in my bedside locker drawer. This Chief told them he was taking the monkey to the Mess to show him off to the guests and would return him afterwards which he had no right to

The China Fleet Club Hong Kong

do. I can only guess as to why these messmates gave him permission and the key.

In the event 'Monk' was wakened late at night in a strange and to him frightening place, It was noisy and he was passed from person to person having his head patted so he must have felt as he did when he was out- side that shop being poked and teased.

Days later I was told what happened next. The band suddenly struck up and apparently 'Monk' 'mustered his kit' all over the lady who was holding him at that moment and doubtless she and her escort beat a hasty retreat.

At the end of my last chapter I referred to an article I had read in the National Newspapers about an incident connected to the Hong Kong Flotilla. It involved an action HMML 1323 had been involved in. When I joined the Flotilla as the Coxswain of HMML 3512, M.L. 1323 had been repaired and was back in the Hong Kong Flotilla. To recall the incident, HMML 1323 had proceeded on a normal three day patrol with her crew of around 13, plus an Army Captain who was accompanying them. They were patrolling down the Pearl River when they encountered a communist gun-craft, which eventually opened fire on them scoring several direct hits in the bridge and wheelhouse areas.

Early on a shell hit the bridge and exploded seriously wounding the C.O. who lost both legs above the knees, and had his right arm smashed and his right hand blown off. He was conscious on the deck for most of what followed but died later on when the launch berthed alongside *H.M.S. Concord.*

Early in the action six crew members and the Army Captain were killed and some of the remaining crew were injured which left Leading Seaman Gordon Cleaver and a couple of other badly shocked crew members to rig emergency steering from the after-end of the M.L. and to keep the engines going until they reached safer waters and were eventually berthed alongside *H.M.S. Concord* who, afterwards towed *M.L. 1323* back to her base at *H.M.S. Tamar*

H.M.M.L. 3512, Hong Kong Flotilla

in Hong Kong. Leading Seaman Cleaver certainly showed great initiative and courage, as did his two helpers, in dealing with the situation they found themselves in and being able to get the badly damaged *M.L. 1323* to safety.

I think I know what they went through during that attack, and I am sure that those events will be fresh in their minds for always.

Leading Seaman Cleaver (20) had done an exceptional job of saving the few survivors of the crew, and the boat, on the 23rd March 1954 he was gazetted with the award of the British Empire Medal, Military Division. In my opinion richly deserved. It is not until we are tested in extraordinary circumstances that we know how we will react as I found on more that one occasion myself and as Leading Seaman Cleaver most probably did.

Hong Kong Flotilla and I parted company after a year and along with several others drafted back to the UK I joined a troopship for the long journey back home. Before I left *H.M.S. Tamar I* was asked by a sailor based there if he could take over the care of 'Monk' and I was happy for him to do so.

Chapter 11

WELL MET

Back in Portsmouth I was sent from RNB to Rosyth Dockyard to stand by *H.M.S. Charity* whilst she underwent an extended refit. Six months later I joined *H.M.S. Excellent* at Whale Island, Portsmouth, to undertake a nine month Gunnery Course for the post of GA 11 (Gun layer/Armourer) which fitted me to join *H.M.S. Woodbridge Haven* in Malta.

This was a quiet number for those who were R.A. and living ashore, but for those among us who were victualled it could become boring after a while for mostly we were secured alongside in Sliema Creek.

I was Captain's Coxswain, which meant looking after his motor boat and attending to his needs. He was a nice man to work with was Captain Dalgleish, very understanding of men, tolerant, and I was lucky for once to serve with such an Officer as he.

Sometimes when I was required to see him in his cabin we would talk about the service or everyday matters, he was particularly keen to know about my wartime experiences, what ships I had served on, and where I had served, what I had done and so on. During one of these chats he asked me what I did off duty, and I explained that I was not all that thrilled with the job because I was about the only non-R.A. in the PO's Mess so usually finished up most nights by being Duty PO. Usually when not on duty I would receive a telephone call which went something like "Ron, would you mind doing Jack a 'sub' (substitute), it's our little girl's birthday and she would love to have her dad at the party too." Most times I would help out by taking the duty but I could not really plan ahead, and anyway

H.M.S. Woodbridge Haven in Malta, 1958

Ship's crew, H.M.S. Woodbridge Haven in Malta, 1958

there was little to plan for if one was not accompanied or didn't have a female friend.

"In other words", said Captain Dalgleish, "you are not happy with your situation here." I agreed that this was true but I qualified this by telling him, "I only have another four months of the commission to do." He then told me that he might be able to get me a more interesting draft but would not promise anything. "Would you like me to try?" he asked, and I said that would be grand, and "Yes, Sir I will gratefully accept your offer."

A week later the Captain told me that "I have a draft for you to *H.M.S. St.Brides Bay* which is based in Singapore, but you would not be leaving us for another two months, how would that suit you?" I thanked him and meant it.

I wondered what lay ahead for me this time in the Far East. A few days after the good news I decided that I had better put my car up for sale and went in to Valetta to place an advert in the *Malta Times*. I chose a Wednesday afternoon to do this, traditionally free for sports in the services, and was about to set off when I spotted our postman about to leave the ship. He was happy to accept a lift to Valetta Post Office where he would collect the ship's mail.

Driving along Manoel Island Road towards Sliema we spotted a 'Jenny Wren' looking splendid in tropical whites, walking some way ahead. I said to 'Posty', "That's unusual, a Jenny on her own. Do you know I've never given a lift to a Wren in this car. I wonder if I can alter that state of affairs." He replied, "Some hope!" Then, "I bet you a 'quid' she refuses." Never one to refuse a challenge, I pulled alongside this gorgeous young lady and chatted to her as she explained that she had just arrived in Malta, "only a few days ago," and was the newest member of her office on Manoel Island. A wedding party had been arranged so she had been given time off to do some shopping. I told her we were going to Valetta and offered her a lift – although at first she didn't seem too keen she eventually accepted.

Jean, my wife, in Malta, 1958

On reaching Valetta shops I parked up and we strolled around the shops in the late afternoon sunshine, completing this with a coffee. I managed to fix a date for that evening and drove her back to her quarters at Whitehall Mansions. I had not got around to advertising the car of course and hung on to it until the day, five weeks later when I left for my new posting.

Jean Watson was eventually to become Jean Walsh and 43 years later thankfully she still is! Naturally, after meeting Jean life became more bearable and interesting as most nights we were out together, except when duty called and *Woodbridge Haven* went to sea on pre-arranged trips.

One such trip took us from Malta, through the Suez Canal to the Gulf of Aquba, as far as Aquba itself (of Lawrence of Arabia fame)

Ship of the desert! Aquaba, Red Sea

and Amman the ancient Jordanian city. We remained there for a week and it proved to be a lovely place, very quiet and isolated. We were anchored just a couple of hundred yards from shore from where the local population took a keen interest in us.

On the third day our First Lieutenant said to me, "The Captain thinks you should come up with something to keep the lads interested. Perhaps shark fishing? There are plenty swimming about here. Naval stores could supply the hooks and I expect the butcher would be able to supply a hunk of meat to use as bait. As for a line I should think the electric winch and the davit will serve that purpose well." I agreed to get everything ready and have a crack at his idea in the morning.

The buzz soon went around the ship and in the morning a sizeable crowd had assembled around the quarter deck to see the PO catch a shark, or worse! I got a couple of the lads to take the winch wire from the electric winch up through a snatch block at the davit head and down to the upper deck where we fixed the huge shark hook with a shackle to the winch line. Now the large lump of meat was pushed over the hook and 'hey-presto' we were ready. The davit was trained outward and the bait lowered until it was under water. When I deemed it sufficiently deep a sudden thrashing, as though all hell had broken loose, erupted from the water, so we let the winch run for a bit and then began heaving it slowly in, the wire being bar tight.

About 12 feet below the surface we could see the head and then as we hauled it out of the water, the body and tail dangling and thrashing about just six feet away from us. It was 10 feet long and dangerous. I thought, what the heck do I do next? Haul it inboard, grab its head under my arm and wrestle it as we tried to extract the hook from its jaws? That was only one solution the crew came up with and there were plenty more, all involving me and not them!

The creature was left dangling while I searched for a workable solution to the dilemma, then the 1st Lt. said, "It looks as if the solution to your problem is about to be solved PO. It would appear that, that lot," he pointed to a bunch of Arabs, "have done it all before and probably in a more serviceable manner than you could". The locals were frantically paddling small boats out towards us intending to take over. After gaining the First's permission we lowered a couple of rope ladders over the side and the shark disposal team clambered aboard. No time was wasted as the shark was brought in board and they cut it up into moveable chunks. The shark teeth were distributed among the lads. We were asked to catch some more of the beasts, but we were not too keen on the idea, although I did agree to one more. It was far too easy to be called a sporting event. No sooner was the bait lowered than a catch was made and this one proved even bigger than the first although the natives were equally as efficient at slicing it up and loading up their boats with the spoils.

Once they had left the ship we rigged hoses and washed the decks. For the next three days we stuck to an upper deck 'Uckers Tournament', and then it was time to up anchor and set off along the Gulf into the Red Sea, up to and through the Suez Canal and back

*Uckers on board H.M.S. Woodbridge Haven, a game for which
the Navy is renowned*

into the Mediterranean Sea and so to return to our base at Malta.
Altogether we had been away for ten days which meant I only had
one week left before leaving the ship to join *H.M.S. St. Brides Bay* in
the Far East. Jean and I had a few days to get to know one another
again.

The day following our return to base I was required in the Captain's
cabin, where he said," Your time is running out PO, are you looking
forward to your new berth in Singapore?" I told him that I had now
found a Wren who seemed to like me and I was certainly over the
moon about her so life had changed for the better somewhat. "In fact
she may be the future Mrs PO Captain's Cox'n, and in fact I was
wondering...!"

"Don't even think about it Cox'n, you just get yo u rself out to the Far
East as I arranged for you and you may find the break will test the
feelings of you both, so have a nice trip and good luck" he said.

At least I had tried and now it was back to RNB Portsmouth to await my flight to Singapore, it wasn't long in coming.

On my arrival there I spent a while in the PO's Mess in *H.M.S.Terror* while *St. Brides Bay* was in temporary refit.

Chapter 12

PAYING OFF

I remained on *H.M.S. St. Brides Bay* in Singapore until my return to the UK in July 1959, and a draft to *H.M.S. Lochinvar* once more to join the Coastal Minesweeper (CMS) *H.M.S. Coniston* as her Coxswain. We were at Port Edgar doing minesweeping and dan laying exercises most of the time. We also visited many foreign ports, among which was Den Helder in Holland, which is the Netherlands Main Naval Base. We also went to Rotterdam, Amsterdam, and the German port of Kiel, as well as many home ports. On board we had 'double L' sweeps (electrical) and the usual Oropesa type.

H.M.S. Coniston was the first of its class of coastal minesweeper and I was the last of its Coxswains as we steamed her down to Chatham Dockyard and paid her off. The following day we commissioned the brand new *H.M.S.Wiston*, also a CMS, and steamed her up to Port Edgar to join the old Flotilla. In May 1960 I left Wiston and went to stay at Jean's home in Blyth, Northumberland, where we married on 14th of that month. In November I flew to Singapore to start a married, accompanied draft in *H.M.S.Terror* Naval Base. My duties were to be in charge of her sailing centre and also be the Captain of *Terror*'s Coxswain.

I was now 40 years old and this was my first married accompanied draft. At first I lived in the PO's Mess and spent my time in *Terror*'s boat shed, some way away from the main part of the base, down beside the river. The building was quite large and I had my office and a living area there for the boat shed crew who were a Leading Seaman, four Royal Navy Able Seamen, six Asian lads, and a C.P.O. Shipwright. Our job was to maintain fourteen R.N.A.S. – 14 foot

H.M.S. Coniston, 1959

H.M.S. Wiston, 1960

dinghy's, re-rigging them, painting and varnishing as required. They were for the use of *H.M.S. Terror's* ships company, or anyone billeted there during ship refits, and so forth.

At the boat shed we had a concrete slipway running straight down to the water so that launching or hauling up boats was no problem.

Another of my responsibilities was the mooring of, fuelling and general care and maintenance of the Captains boat, a 30-footer with a single inboard engine and canvas canopy over the wheel and half upper deck. It was ideal, and only used for, 'banyans (picnics) up river. The Captain did not use his boat very often and had told me that when he did not require it at weekends I could make use of it for organising banyan parties. I recall that we had around four while I was there.

The we ather was hot in Singapore but we had a good work routine and great team. At about 300 yards along the river bank from the boat house was another, most impressive building in the oriental style. It has a red painted pagoda roof and was always called the 'Red House'. It was single floored in which was a large room with three other smaller office-like ones leading off from it. This was where the office of my immediate boss, the Warrant Officer Shipwright, was situated. Besides being responsible for the boat shed he also had other duties.

We heard plenty of tales from the Asian wo r k e rs about what the Red House and the boat shed were used for by the Japanese during their occupation of Singapore in WWII.

After two months my wife joined me and we hired a bungalow in

H.M.S. Terror naval base boat shed

H.M.S. Terror Singapore

Ron and pal outside the Red House

Jalon Kemuning, Sembuang village near the main entrance road to
H.M.S. Terror. This was to be a temporary accommodation until
something more suitable could be found in married quarter, but we
liked it so much that we stayed. There were other naval families living around us and it was convenient living 'outside the gate'.

We left Singapore and flew home to the UK on 22nd February

1963. During our stay in Singapore our son was born just nine months before we came home and my 22 years engagement with the Navy was due to expire, in four months time. I made a request to sign on for a '5th five' which was granted by *H.M.S.Error's* Captain.

After a few days leave I went to *H.M.S. Excellent* (Whale Island) for a refresher course in gunnery and afterwards received a very nice draft to *H.M.S. Unicorn* in Dundee, Scotland. Which was another married accompanied tour where both my wife and son could join me as soon as a quarter could be arranged.

H.M.S. Unicorn was, and still is as far as I know, the oldest warship afloat having been launched in Chatham in 1824 and placed in 'mothballs' to be used as a 'powder hulk' on the Medway and Thames until 1873 when she was towed to Dundee to become the navy's training ship for the area. I joined her as a Petty Officer Seamanship Instructor for the R.N.V.R. (Royal Naval Volunteer Reserve). *Unicorn* didn't go anywhere, she was secured alongside. The Captain was a local businessman and the 1st Lieutenant was a Lt. Cmdr. RN., p e rmanently employed on board. He was my boss.

H.M.S. Unicorn

The job was pleasant and straightforwa r d , instructing classes of RNVR's mostly in the evenings and at weekends. At the start Jean and our son and I shared a large house in Carnoustie, near Dundee, divided into two flats which were naval hiring's. It was a good hiring as it overlooked the golf course and had the sea behind it. Unfortunately, after a couple of months the place developed hot water boiler trouble and then the boiler over the bath caught fire just as I was bathing our son one evening. An inspection by navy social services decided that the place was not suitable and we were moved to a nice bungalow at nearby Broughty Ferry. We soon settled in and everything went along very nicely for a few months.

When I had joined *Unicorn* I had been told by the Captain that I would be with him for 18 months, so I was somewhat surprised when nine months later he sent for me and dropped the bombshell that I would be going on an unaccompanied draft to Bahrain in the Persian Gulf where I was to join *H.M.S. Anzio,* a Tank Landing Craft (TLC) as Chief Bosun's Mate.

Before I could express my views he explained that I was being offered the draft which I could turn down if I wanted to, but he went on that the job required a Chief Petty Officer and that if I accepted it then I would be rated up when my 'B31' arrived at the ship. "The choice is yours PO." What a dilemma. He went on, "Let me know what you decide when you come in on Monday."

Jean and I talked it over and decided that it would be silly to let the chance go, so after the weekend I told the 1st. Lt. that I would accept the draft. He agreed that it was a wise decision because I would be changing a cushy number but would be getting Chief's rate faster than otherwise, and that meant a higher pension, etc. The situation was more disconcerting because our daughter, Karen, who was born in our comfy bungalow on the 18th April 1964 was only a couple of months old.

We packed our belongings, surrendered the bungalow, and travelled

146

A tank going through the bow-doors to the deck inside, H.M.S. Anzio 1964

by car to Jean's parents in Blyth on 2nd June 1964, and just 10 days later I boarded a plane and flew to join *H.M.S. Anzio*, attached to *H.M.S. Jufair*, the Royal Navy base at Bahrain. Crewing a tank landing craft was a new experience for me and was most enjoyable all the time I was aboard her, until paying her off at Gibraltar. At Jufair there was a long, strongly bu i l t, concrete jetty with mooring facilities enabling ships small or large to berth on either side. It was very hot and we wore tropical rig at all times. D u ring the first few months I was there we ferried troops and their vehicles to various isolated stretches of desert along the Pe rsian Gulf, where we disembarked them and awaited their return after they had conducted their manoeuvres and exercises in the sands. Sometimes we were away for days, especially when we were around the Aden area. Then it was load up and steam back to Bahrain.

When an exercise was about to start all the Army tanks and heavy vehicles would come down the jetty and be loaded on to our tank deck. The Army personnel would settle themselves on the upper deck. I soon got used to the routine on board, maintaining good ru n-ning of upper deck work and smooth running of the day to day duties at sea and in harbour, plus supervision of work of the two watches. I was victualled in the Petty Officer Mess with five others

147

H.M.S. Anzio

but I expected to move into the CPO's Mess in short order when my 'B31' came through. This was the official form of authority that arrives when a rating is due for promotion. He would be advised to attend the Captain's Request men to be rated up.

Our first exercise was about to take place and I found that my duties changed to the tank deck which was directly below the upper deck and on ground level so that tanks and vehicles could drive straight on via the open bow-doors. For the duration of the exercise a Royal Navy Captain came aboard from *H.M.S. Jufair* to oversee, and be in charge of, the safe loading and disembarking, and re-loading of the Army vehicular equipment. My job was to work closely with him while he was on board.

The exercise was straightforward from our point of view. It was always hot and sultry weather and with our bow-doors open and ramp down the lorries would be driven in along each side and the tanks in the middle to give stability. The tanks would leave the ship first either onto the beach or via a 'Rhino' barge of the type

H.M.S. Anzio
Left: Chief Shipwright and myself; right: Chief Stoker and myself
(Coxswain in the background)

H.M.S. Anzio
The Chief Bosun's Mate

developed for the D-day landings in Normandy during WWII. Usually they went straight from the ships ramp to the beach after we had pushed into the waters edge with bow doors open and ramp down. If the beach didn't shelve and the tanks might sink that was when the 'Rhino' barge was used. This was simply a long metal raft that could be floated between ship and beach!

Once the Army had gone off into the desert we were free to resume our normal duties. More often than not we would sit around in groups discussing current events during tea or coffee breaks. At such times my boss of the moment, the RN Captain, would retire to the Wardroom. Occasionally we would chat about ships we had served in and experiences that had happened to us. He used to like to steer the conversation around to WWII and it certainly passed the time and made the sea days up and down the Gulf, and even as far as Aden at the southern end of the Red Sea, a lot more interesting.

After that first exercise, about two weeks after I had joined the ship I was cooling off in the evening on the upper deck when our Chief Writer, a CPO, joined me and told me on the quiet that my B31 had arrived on board and I could, therefore, expect to join their mess in a few days when the coxswain would tell me to attend Captain's Request men. That little bit of information was, of course, told in confidence from one senior rate to another and was the way information was generally confided.

It so happened that I was not told to see the Captain as I expected but we did another exercise which lasted ten days and it was a week after that when I was eventually told to attend request men.

Once I was in front of him the Captain got right down to business and said "Petty Officer, your B31 is on board but I do not intend to rate you up. I am not prepared to recommend you so I will be returning the B31!" He asked if I had anything to say to that end, but the wind had been taken from my sails so I replied, "No, Sir, but can I now expect to be drafted off this ship and back to the UK when my

*An A.B. and myself on the ramp waiting for the 'Rhino' to
come back with the tanks*

*One of the tanks (eight in all) about to go on board through the bow-doors,
H.M.S. Anzio*

relief comes on board?" He then told me he was satisfied with my
work on board as Chief Bosun's Mate so that he would expect me to
continue those duties for the rest of the commission. With that he
dismissed me!

151

So it was back to the PO's Mess and make the best of it or I could put in a request for a draft. However, doing it from the ship would probably become a long drawn out affair so I decided to take it on the chin and carry on to the standards I had always set myself.

The next exercise was a long one. We steamed down the Gulf of Oman along the south coast of Saudi Arabia to Aden. After a week there we set off on the return journey to Bahrain with another full day of exercises on the beach in the Gulf, not far from Bahrain. It was during that one-day exercise that my boss and I got chatting over a cup of tea whilst waiting to embark the Army. He told me that we would not be there much longer. Then he said, "I am curious to know why you are still a P.O. Chief Bosun's Mate instead of a CPO. Is there any good reason for it?" Then I told him that I had been sent to the ship to pick up my B31 but had just been told by the CO that he was not going to recommend me, though he was very satisfied with my work. He, the Captain, simply said, "Is that so!"

The following morning was a busy one. We berthed alongside the Bahrain Mole early on the Saturday morning then we had the bustle of unloading the tanks, lorries and soldiers when the RN Captain said to me "See you next trip, Buffer." and he left to return to *H.M.S. Jufair.* After clearing up and washing the decks it was down to the Mess to scrub out and get ready for 'Mess deck Rounds' by the CO. I heard a while after that that our CO had been requested to make a visit to someone at the base and that he had put back 'Captains Rounds' by nearly an hour. Perhaps that visit had some connection to the later event which took place that morning. After rounds the Cox'n came to see me and told me to get into No 1 uniform and be up on the bridge by 12.15pm.

I was put in front of the CO, who simply said "Rated Chief Petty Officer as from (the date of my B31 coming on board the ship), dismissed!" Just like that. No fuss, no apology, no explanation.

I continued doing my job during the commission and then came the

'Esso Norway' aground and on fire in the Gulf, salvaged by H.M.S. Anzio and towed to port for repair

long trip home.

D u ring one occasion in the Gulf we came across a tanker on fire and a ground at the wat e rs edge. It did not appear to be a big fire though there was plenty of smoke. With our shallow draft we were able to get alongside and put on a boarding party consisting of the First Lieutenant, myself, and half a dozen lads. The *Esso Norway* had evidently been abandoned so our First took charge of her. We rigged up hoses and directed a good flow of water down her after hatch from which the smoke appeared to be issuing forth. By then it was late evening so a watch rota was set up which meant that an eye could be kept on her all the way through the dark hours. The following day a line was rigged up from the tankers stem and Anzio went astern herself, the *Esso Norway* coming off the beach quite easily. Once afloat we re-rigged the tow-line and took her to a pre-arranged place to tum her over to tugs. It was almost evening by the time we tied up at Bahrain and almost two years later when I received £75 salvage money.

Eventually we set off on the long trip home, made longer by the fact that our cruising speed was around 10 knots, through the Gulf of Oman into the Arabian Sea and onto Bombay, gateway to India, where she went into dry-dock for a routine inspection. Two weeks later we were at sea again and heading for the beautiful Seychelles in the Indian Ocean. The main island was an ideal holiday destination with long sandy beaches and plenty of sunshine to lap up while lazing upon them. The only drawback for most visiting ships was the shallow water around the island which meant they had to anchor offshore and liberty boats had to be used to ferry them back and forth to the long jetty which ran well out into the sea. Our shallow draft allowed us to tie up right next to the shore part of the jetty, open the bow doors and let down the ramp so that we could walk on and off the ship at our leisure.

Ten days later we were off again, heading for the East Coast of Africa, and Bombay once again where we stayed a week and then headed up to the Gulf of Aden once more with a short stop at Djibouti before greeting the Red Sea and Suez Canal like old friends. In the Med again we sailed to Gibraltar and docked. Here we paid off the commission and flew back to the UK. After an eventful and interesting year in Anzio I was once more entering the RNB drafting office at Portsmouth.

H.M.S. Excellent, where I was to spend two years as Chief of the Footbridge, sharing with another Chief Petty Officer was my first major security job. We had a small staff responsible for everyone who entered and left Whale Island. It was a watch-keeping job because we had to man the bridge day and night, which suited me fine as I now lived in Fareham which meant a straight run from work every day. Eventually drafting office caught up with me once more.

In early September 1967 I flew out to Bermuda to join *H.M.S. Lynx*, a Leopard Class type 41 anti-aircraft frigate far removed from the old anti-aircraft ship I first joined so long ago, *H.M.S. Foylebank*. She was half-way through a South American commission when I joined her to relieve her CBM who was making an early return to the UK. I would serve the latter half of the commission. The ship was mainly based in Bermuda and the routine then was that from Monday to Friday afternoons we would carry out Cuba patrols and then visit in turn the Florida towns of Key-West, Miami, and Fort Lauderdale. During my time with *H.M.S. Lynx* everything worked out as a pleasant berth for me as well as being the last sea-going ship I served in.

Early in 1968 we steamed her back to the UK and docked at her home Devonport where we paid her off then it was back to Pompey for me to join the cruiser *H.M.S. Belfast* which was then moored at Whale Island serving as Base Ship.

My last few months in the Royal Navy were as Chief of a patrol party consisting of myself, a Leading Seaman, and two Able Seamen. Our job was to make daily inspections of the reserve ships moored in the upper reaches of Fareham Creek. There were aircraft carriers, frigates, destroyers, cruisers, submarines, etc., and many of them had famous war records, but none were needed any more and were indeed 'up the creek'.

These ships were a great attraction being full of brass parts and various collectable items such as bells, compasses and so on. Undesirable types were already boarding them and removing what they could get into small boats. Anything that would move or could be moved were being stripped. Sometimes we came across serious vandalism which had to be stopped and the damage repaired by skilled craftsmen from the dockyard who we would ferry across and wait while they carried out their task. As some ships could be sold to foreign navies they had to be of a certain standard, and it was my job to see that they were while I was still in the navy. It was very eerie on those silent, dark ships where the only light came from our torches, and it was easy to get lost, as some of our party found out. We would collect at the entrance and then fan out and look for the missing man.

On 28th April 1969 I was discharged from the Royal Navy and had to find something to do as a civilian. I had registered with the Labour Office in Fareham, and told them I was having two weeks leave before starting work. However, a week later I received a phone call informing me that a job was available at the nearby base *H.M.S. Collingwood*, right on my doorstep. If I had a driving licence the civilian transport section was looking for a driver. Presenting myself at the main gate as instructed I had an interview with the section chargeman, a test drive in a 30 seater coach followed, and I was offered the job. I started a week later near the end of June 1969.

In those days we had two coaches, two Ford TK lorries, a fire-engine, an ambulance, three Tilleys and a staff car. Our maintenance needs were catered for at the large transport section at H.MS. Daedalus. During 15 years as an employee, most of them as a driver, my last two were spent in the base Armoury as a member of the workshop's maintenance party. I finally retired from *H.M.S. Collingwood* in 1984.

Appendix 1

SHIPS/SHORE ESTABLISHMENTS WHERE SERVED

PEMBROKE from 20/11/36
WILDFIRE from 27/02/37
IRON DUKE from 15/06/37
GLASGOW from 14/09/37
VICTORY from 16/04/40
FOYLEBANK from 30/05/40
VICTORY from 05/07/40
BULLDOG from 12/09/40
WINDSOR from 15/04/41
VICTORY from 03/06/42
OSPREY from 05/06/42
ACUTE from 10/07/42
VICTORY from 07/07/43
SAKER USN from 21/10/43
KINGSMILL from 06/12/43
NIMROD from 16/09/44
OSPREY from 25/11/44
BRISSENDEN from 21/12/44
OSPREY from 19/06/45
VICTORY from 08/09/45
COLLINGWOOD from 16/04/46
MTB5003 from 14/11/46
HORNET from 01/04/47
VICTORY from 28/06/47
SISKIN from 25/09/47
CONDOR from 07/02/48
DAEDALUS from 08/04/49

VICTORY from 03/03/52
LOCHINVAR from 20/05/52
CREOLE from 06/02/53
VICTORY from 01/09/53
BOXER from 09/10/53
TAMAR from 01/04/55
VICTORY from 27/05/56
CHARITY from 27/07/56
EXCELLENT from 01/02/57
WOODBRIDGE HAVEN from 14/02/58
VICTORY from 23/12/58
ST BRIDES BAY from 23/01/59
LOCHINVAR   from 22/07/59
CONISTON from 02/03/60
WISTON from 12/04/60
LOCHINVAR from 07/11/60
TERROR from 30/11/60
VICTORY from 22/02/63
EXCELLENT from 22/04/63
UNICORN from 03/07/63
ANZIO from 18/05/64
VICTORY from 23/05/65
EXCELLENT from 28/06/65
LYNX from 09/09/67
BELLEROPHON from 18/01/68
VICTORY from 18/03/69

SOME SHIPS SERVED ON

H.M.S. Brissenden, December 1944–June 1945

H.M.S. Hornet, Gosport, November 1946–June 1947

H.M.S. St. Brides Bay, 1959

Appendix 3

THE WALSH BROTHERS

Bob Walsh

Fred Walsh (on left)

Ron Walsh

John Walsh

Appendix 4

H.M.S. COLLINGWOOD

Transport drivers at H.M.S. Collingwood, 1967

Transport drivers at H.M.S. Collingwood, 1980

H.M.S. Collingwood Armoury Staff, 1983

A well-earned retirement

RONALD David Walsh, age 64, has retired from HMS Collingwood, the Royal Naval School of Weapon Engineering in Fareham.

He has been employed at the establishment since 1969, when he left the Royal Navy.

He started as a transport driver where he remained until 1983. After that he spent a short time in the armoury, went back for a while to transport and finished his time as a member of the maintenance party in the workshops.

Ronald met his wife Jean in Malta in 1958, when she was a Leading Wren (Victualling). They married in May 1960 and now live in St. Annes Grove, Fareham. They have two children, Karen (19) who works at Admiralty Service Weapons Establishment, and David (21) who is employed in the building trade.

Ronald intends to spend his retirement maintaining the cars that his family have gathered together—there are upwards of eight at any

one time.

During the war years, Ronald wrote many poems and collated them into a book with illustrations, which a touching and personal view of active service at that time. Many were accepted for publication during the war and tell of events that affected the lives of sailors in the Royal Navy of 40 years ago.

Mr. Walsh is pictured with the Captain of HMS Collingwood, Captain Anthony Wheatley.

VC's courage inspires today's gunners

● *Princess Anne with Foylebank veterans Doug Bishop (left) and Jack Wheeler. They were accompanied by Mrs Myra Bishop (centre) veteran Ron Walsh, Mrs Jean Walsh and Jack Wheeler's daughter Mrs Ruth Goodenough.*

THE COURAGE of a WWII gunner is inspiring a new generation of sailors at HMS Collingwood.

Leading Seaman Jack Mantle was awarded a posthumous Victoria Cross for his defence of the armed merchant cruiser HMS Foylebank during a devastating air attack by German dive bombers at Portland in July 1940.

And his name lives on at the Fareham establishment where a new close-range weapons trainer has been named in his honour .

Jack was due to be mentioned in despatches for an earlier action when he brought down an enemy aircraft with a Lewis gun, but he was mortally wounded during the attack on the Foylebank.

He was wounded many times and had time to reflect on his grievous injuries between bursts of fire, but his courage bore him up until the end of the fight when he fell by his gun.

During a visit to the new trainer by the Princess Royal, Princess

● *LS Jack Mantle, VC.*

Anne met survivors of the attack on the Foylebank.

Doug Bishop, Chairman of the HMS Foylebank Association, said: "The idea is that people going on the course will be inspired by Jack's example. His courage shows them what they have to live up to."

H.R.H. Princess Royal opens the H.M.S. Collingwood 'Mantle Room' 2001

H.M.S. Foylebank survivors.
From left, Jack Wheeler, Ron Walsh and Doug Bishoip